DARK SAYINGS
Diary of an American Priest

DARK SAYINGS
Diary of an American Priest

Marc Philip Boulos

OCABS PRESS
ST PAUL, MINNESOTA 55124
2023

DARK SAYINGS
Diary of an American Priest

Copyright © 2023 by
Marc Philip Boulos

ISBN 1-60191-056-8

All rights reserved.

PRINTED IN THE UNITED STATES OF AMERICA

Dark Sayings
Diary of an American Priest

Copyright © 2023 by Marc Philip Boulos
All rights reserved.

ISBN 1-60191-056-8

Published by OCABS Press, St. Paul, Minnesota.
Printed in the United States of America.

Books are available through OCABS Press at special discounts for bulk purchases in the United States by academic institutions, churches, and other organizations. For more information, please email OCABS Press at press@ocabs.org.

Cover design by Daliya[1] Boulos.

---

[1] In Arabic, a grapevine. In Hebrew, a gentle or slender branch or tendril on the Lord's mighty cedar, under which "birds of every kind will nest" and find shade: *"All the trees of the field will know that I am the Lord; I bring down the high tree, exalt the low tree, dry up the green tree, and make the dry tree flourish. I am the Lord; I have spoken, and I will perform it."* (Ezekiel 17:22-24)

To Paul and Rose

"A Maskil ("wise teaching") of Asaph.
Listen, O my people, to my instruction (torah);
Incline your ears to the words of my mouth.
I will open my mouth in a parable (mashal);
I will utter dark sayings (hidot) of old,
Which we have heard and known,
And our fathers have told us.

We will not conceal them from their children,
But tell to the generation to come the praises of the Lord,
His strength and his wondrous works that he has done.

For he established a testimony in Jacob
And appointed a law in Israel,
Which he commanded our fathers
That they should teach them to their children,
That the generation to come might know, even the children yet to be born.

That they may arise and tell them to their children,
That they should put their confidence in God
And not forget the works of God,
But keep his commandments,
And not be like their fathers,
A stubborn and rebellious generation,
A generation that did not prepare its heart
And whose spirit was not faithful to God."

(Psalm 78:1-8)

Preface

The Hebrew words *hidah* (riddle, dark saying) and *mashal* (allegory, parable) are different but close enough in their biblical usage[2] that the difference need not be stressed:

> *"Son of man (*ben 'adam*), riddle a riddle (*hud hidah*) and parable a parable (*meshol mashal*) to the house (*el-bayt*) of Israel." (Ezekiel 17:2)*

In both Ezekiel and Psalm 78, the Riddler's Parable is a test, a puzzle, a *maskil* (wise teaching) for the disciple, not to interpret, but to work at, work out, and hopefully, make functional in daily life. The latter can only be done through persistence, under the constant pressure of Elohim's judgment, for "wisdom," the Preacher explains, illumines the wise man "and causes his stern face to beam." (Ecclesiastes 8:1) Such a man:

> *"Keep[s] the command of the king because of the oath before God." (Ecclesiastes 8:2)*

In this spirit, the enclosed sermons are a collection of dark sayings, a diary, not of my personal experience, but of the work of God's *maskil* in the daily life of priestly ministry channeled through biblical preaching.

Such riddles are difficult and time-consuming. Even in the original languages, where the text is plain, the biblical riddle demands to be searched. While (or

---

[2] Tarazi, Paul N. *The Chrysostom Bible - Ezekiel: A Commentary*. OCABS Press, 2012, p. 210.

Preface

perhaps because) people roll their eyes and scratch their heads at Elohim's *ḥidah*, Jesus challenges us:

"Seek, and ye shall find; knock, and it shall be opened to you." (Matthew 7:7)

In Hebrew, the word *darash* (search, study) is a double-edged sword. As you search, you imagine that you are studying Scripture when in truth, the Scriptural God studies *you*. Only when it is too late do you discover the truth: that you have followed in the footsteps of your fathers, the very fathers to whom God entrusted the Torah you now hold in your sinful hands. But they did not follow it, and now *they are gone*. To make matters worse, you picked up the same *maskil*, only to discover that *you* yourself *did not follow it*, and now *you* are under the same condemnation.[3]

That riddle is the kernel (Greek *kokkos*) of the biblical *debarim* (words) of Elohim. More than roll their eyes, faced with this puzzle, people in the parishes would rather hurl insults at the preacher and "wag their heads" (Matthew 27:39) than face the painful honesty of the gospel.

Itself a microcosm of the biblical storyline, Psalm 78 begins after the pattern of Genesis, which demotes, *even subjugates*, humanity (*ha 'adam*). Its premise is Yahweh, our Elohim, who, akin to a Roman Patrician, cares for his people for the sake of *his own honor*, despite their

---

[3] "When the king heard the words of the book of the law, he tore his clothes." (2 Kings 22:11)

constant misdeeds, betrayals, and failures. He does so through David, his *locum tenens:*

> *"Then the Lord awoke as if from sleep, like a warrior overcome by wine…He also chose David, his slave, and took him from the sheepfolds; From the care of the ewes with suckling lambs, he brought him to shepherd Jacob, his people, and Israel, his inheritance. So, he shepherded them according to the integrity of his heart and guided them with his skillful hands." (Psalm 78:65,70-72)*

Unfortunately, David and those who followed after him failed. They trusted in themselves and the work of their own hands. As such, the biblical story of their reign unfolds as a dark saying (*hidah*), a *mashal*, wisdom as a cautionary tale, a parabolic example of what not to do.

Beginning with Saul, the line of biblical kings ends in ashes and exile—as did any attempts at restoration. In the eyes of the Scriptural God, Hegel and his ilk were wrong. There is no process of development, let alone human progress, individual or collective. We human beings are no better than our parents. We do not even measure up.

Under such pressure—the weight (*kabod*) of biblical instruction—our best hope is to submit to God, our heavenly Father, grasping not at our strength but trusting in *his* wisdom, according to the integrity of *his* heart, guided by *his* skillful hands.

—Marc Philip Boulos

Table of Contents

Preface	13
Table of Contents	17
Dark Sayings: Diary of an American Priest	19
The Refugee Church	*19*
The Tribal Patriarch	*28*
In God's Hands	*33*
The Pearl of Great Price	39
A Church History Lesson	49
Bow or Walk Away	53
Why I Do Not Vote	*54*
A Mental Vacancy	63
Open the Eyes of Your Mind	*64*
Heritage is Not Ancestral	71
God Does Not Need Your Bread	*72*
No Security Blankets	77
The Voice of the Shepherd	*78*
I Believe in One God	89
Call No Human Being Your Father	*90*
Glorify Your Father and Mother	*98*
The *Toledot* of Elohim	109
Whom We Do Not See	*110*
Understanding Irrelevance	121
Grasshoppers	*122*
In the Wilderness	127
A House of Cedar?	*129*
Son of Man	145
The Challenge	*147*
Stand Your Ground	163
In Memory of Daniel del Castillo	*166*
Bread and Stone	185
Dung Piles	*186*

Dark Sayings: Diary of an American Priest

The Refugee Church

"I come from there, and I have memories
Born as mortals are, I have a mother
And a house with many windows,
I have brothers, friends,
And a prison cell with a cold window."
   —Mahmoud Darwish, I Come From There

I grew up in a Palestinian refugee camp in Minnesota on St. Paul's West Side. Like many around the world, my childhood community was a coincidence of civil war. In my case, multiple wars. My mother's family fled conflict in the Middle East when she was a toddler. My father abandoned his beloved Egypt in the aftermath of the Six-Day War. My parents courted each other at the center of our camp, which revolved around our family church. Like its members—an eclectic assortment of immigrants, refugees, and Americans—our church was itself a refugee, separated by strife from a neighboring immigrant parish, hidden between the lines of political divisions in the national church.

Our pastor, my grandfather, lost his homeland, property, friends, honor, and his priestly ministry in a neighboring church. The last blow was the most painful. Homeless and jobless, he and my grandmother opted to remain in Minnesota to provide stability for their children. He found menial work during the week as a janitor and celebrated the liturgy with his immediate family at our church on Sundays.

The Refugee Church

The broader community shunned our family and refugee church. Then and now, people criticize my childhood church calling it "dysfunctional." What they mean is that the tribal norms of communal, nomadic cultures are incompatible with their Melting Pot. Before they employed the term dysfunctional, the colonials referred to nomadic peoples like the Native Americans as savages. Yes, we are savages. A transient community organized around the authority of a tribal chief who does not yield to the institutional norms of Western society—people who eat with their hands—terrifies them.

I am thankful to James Baldwin, who exposed the Melting Pot to me as a fake baptismal font, where Americans fondle each other in a desperate attempt to erase their sins against people of color by erasing color. Instead of giving way to the Melting Pot, I pursued my interest in my culture and religion. I studied Arabic and, before attending seminary, made my first visit to the Middle East. My experience of nomadic hospitality, community, and human connection was path-altering, as was my encounter with Zionism and Christian sectarianism. The absurdity of competing claims on the land and its shrines almost pushed me away from religion, pulling the first thread in my eventual deconstruction.

Unlike nomadic societies, institutionalized and colonial America is dependent on "community builders" to maintain the illusion of fellowship. The phrase community builder is useful for describing anyone who believes that an institution, properly organized and maintained, can be a healthy, scalable,

Dark Sayings

functional neighborhood. Such people are the builders of barns (Luke 12:18) who trust in the work of their own hands, undoing the work of God's hands. Horrifically, their philosophical belief is codified in American law, which now assigns "personhood" to corporations.[4] And what is the outcome of all this? American community builders dismantled the family farm and family businesses, stripping rural communities of their livelihood. In their place, they erected large franchises and department stores. Their creations destroyed and supplanted the families and neighborhoods God himself forms in the womb. In the eyes of such builders, micro-communities are easily dismissed because they are unscalable. In their rush to build and expand, they never stop to consider that their way of thinking and speaking is strictly prohibited in the New Testament. Luke disallows expansion (Luke 12:16–21), and Matthew stands out in his critique of human judgment (Matthew 7:1).

Looking back as an adult, I realize I grew up in such a micro-community and loved it. My grandparents were simple people. For all their flaws, they managed to bottle a moment in time, making the breathable air of 1940s Palestine functional in our West Side lungs. Running under pressure in their shadow from conflict and shame, my participation in the Orthodox Church began as a mix of pride, nostalgia, and alienation from the center. In an era when religion and my Arab roots remain the

---

[4] Wikipedia contributors. "Santa Clara County V. Southern Pacific Railroad Co." *Wikipedia*, Apr. 2023, en.wikipedia.org/wiki/Santa_Clara_County_v._Southern_Pacific_Railroad_Co.

The Refugee Church

butt of the joke, I was proud to be an Arab and Orthodox. Three gifts sustained me then and now: a powerful ego, my father's persistent criticism of Western culture, and a deeply ingrained disregard for the opinions of others.

Like all human dung piles, our family's camp was useful for a time and useful when it was gone. Whether made by the hand of man or born of a mother's womb, all institutions are temporary. We were an unscalable, transient refugee church. Like Palestine, our little community—the homeland of my childhood formation—suffered total and complete destruction.

At a time when the threat of invading enemies was constant, the authors of the Bible took the novel approach of resisting their conquerors through *total self-condemnation*. Themselves the children of an advanced society,[5] these writers filled the pages of Scripture with

---

[5] One need only read the "Darius Naqsh-e Rostam" inscription "a" from the tomb of Darius the Great (490 BC, nearly two millenia after Sargon founded the kingdom of Sumer and Akkad in 2334 BC) to capture the "smallness" of Alexander the "great" in the eyes of the biblical authors and, at the same time, the mentality of Psalm 78 and Scripture as a whole, which opted for self-condemnation to undermine the arrogance of their silly "conquering" children: "A great god is Ahuramazda, who created this earth, who created yonder sky, who created man, who created happiness for man, who made Darius king, one king of many, one lord of many. I am Darius the great king, king of kings, king of countries containing all kinds of men, king in this great earth far and wide, son of Hystaspes, an Achaemenid, a Persian, son of a Persian, an Aryan, having Aryan lineage. King Darius says: By the favor of Ahuramazda these are the countries which I seized outside of Persia; I ruled over them;

Dark Sayings

the relentless denunciation of cities and human civilization:

> *"I will make Jerusalem a heap of ruins, a haunt of jackals; And I will make the cities of Judah a desolation, without inhabitant. Who is the wise man that may understand this? And who is he to whom the mouth of the Lord has spoken, that he may declare it? Why is the land ruined, laid waste*

---

they bore tribute to me; they did what was said to them by me; they held my law firmly; Media, Elam, Parthia, Aria, Bactria, Sogdia, Chorasmia, Drangiana, Arachosia, Sattagydia, Gandara [Gadâra], India [Hiduš], the haoma-drinking Scythians, the Scythians with pointed caps, Babylonia, Assyria, Arabia, Egypt, Armenia, Cappadocia, Lydia, the Greeks (Yauna), the Scythians across the sea (Sakâ), Thrace, the petasos-wearing Greeks [Yaunâ], the Libyans, the Nubians, the men of Maka and the Carians. King Darius says: Ahuramazda, when he saw this earth in commotion, thereafter, bestowed it upon me, made me king; I am king. By the favor of Ahuramazda I put it down in its place; what I said to them, that they did, as was my desire. If now you shall think that 'How many are the countries which King Darius held?' look at the sculptures [of those] who bear the throne, then shall you know, then shall it become known to you: the spear of a Persian man has gone forth far; then shall it become known to you: a Persian man has delivered battle far indeed from Persia. Darius the King says: This which has been done, all that by the will of Ahuramazda I did. Ahuramazda bore me aid, until I did the work. May Ahuramazda protect me from harm, and my royal house, and this land: this I pray of Ahuramazda, this may Ahuramazda give to me! O man, that which is the command of Ahuramazda, let this not seem repugnant to you; do not leave the right path; do not rise in rebellion!"; Wikipedia contributors. "DNa Inscription." *Wikipedia*, Aug. 2023, en.wikipedia.org/wiki/DNa _inscription.; Wikipedia contributors. "King of Sumer and Akkad." *Wikipedia*, May 2023, en.wikipedia.org/wiki/King_of_Sumer_and_Akkad.

The Refugee Church

> *like a desert, so that no one passes through? The Lord said, "Because they have forsaken my law which I set before them, and have not obeyed my voice nor walked according to it, but have walked after the stubbornness of their heart and after the Baals, as their fathers taught them," therefore thus says the Lord of hosts, the God of Israel, "behold, I will feed them, this people, with wormwood and give them poisoned water to drink. I will scatter them among the nations, whom neither they nor their fathers have known; and I will send the sword after them until I have annihilated them." (Jeremiah 9:11–16)*

The example from Jeremiah reflects a consistent point throughout the biblical storyline: obedience to God's law in opposition to the plurality of human wisdoms. As the child of immigrants, I was subjected to the supposed wisdom of the American way. However, of far greater importance, when Scripture deals with human wisdom, it addresses that of the institutionalized Greeks, the architects of the classical world.

A thousand years before the birth of Greek philosophy, the forbears of the biblical authors inhabited a world in which the families of the earth coexisted in the land with different languages and cultures. No melting pots. I hesitate to use the word "identity" because, for my readers, it is a philosophical term. As sons and daughters of Plato and Aristotle, *identity* operates as a concept or construction of your minds. In the historical setting of the Old Testament, the authors' focus was not on identity, but *locality*, the place where you are found.

Dark Sayings

Using the lens of language, food, clothing, skin color, economic or social status, beliefs, music, and other passing characteristics, community builders apply identity as a powerful tool for social organization. Whether Greek conquerors or modern Americans, community builders depend on philosophical identity because the nature of their colonial project is to overrun and control locality. Philosophical identity is the cause of all man-made suffering.

Whereas the Bible ridicules cities filled with artificial and lifeless statues, this is simply an older version of modern cynicism about cheap plastic products. Hearing this, it is hard not to shudder at the idea of assigning a personality to the institutions that Americans fashion with their own hands:

> *"They have mouths, but they do not speak; They have eyes, but they do not see; They have ears, but they do not hear, Nor is there any breath at all in their mouths. Those who make them will become like them, yes, everyone who trusts in them."*
> *(Psalm 135:16–18)*

Through Scripture, *you* and the tribe in which God makes you his son or daughter are under the judgment of his law. *You*, not your enemies, must obey his voice or suffer the consequences enumerated in Jeremiah and elsewhere. *You* must care for others who dwell in and near the locality in which *you* are found:

> *"For the whole law is fulfilled in one word, in the statement, "YOU SHALL LOVE YOUR NEIGHBOR AS YOURSELF." But if you bite and devour one another, take*

The Refugee Church

care that you are not consumed by one another." (Galatians 5:14)

In Scripture, the word "neighbor," like my use of the term identity, is not philosophical. To a practical (non-Hellenized) person, the phrase "Who is my neighbor?" (Luke 10:29) is a stupid question. Luke's parable of the Samaritan presents your neighbor as the person in physical proximity to you when you walk along the road. The Old Testament places the other families dwelling in your locality as your neighbor. In the example from Galatians, Paul is writing to other families in and near his locality. Your tribe and family—the Prophets repeatedly warn—cannot exist for themselves. *It is not your family, but the law of God set before you that is exceptional.* This law pushes you toward coexistence with your neighbor in the condition in which you found them. "Each man," Paul explains, "must remain in that condition in which he was called." (1 Corinthians 7:20) Whether at the center of man-made civilization or on the outside, you may not impose anything on those living next to you, and you may not export your colonial brand. James Baldwin got it right, "People aren't meant to be melted [they] don't want to be melted down. They

Dark Sayings

resist it with all their strength."[6] The colonial Melting Pot is anti-Scriptural.[7]

Community builders think that right-minded beliefs, values, cultures, ideas, processes, operating procedures, principles, structures, visions, and goals differentiate modern institutions from the tribal camp of my youth. They believe that something packaged and labeled is better than something homemade. They worship a standard of their making, a correct and scalable model to be instituted, boxed, franchised, and imposed on everyone outward from their artificial center. To the extent that God raised Jesus from the dead, they are desperate to raise their alternative, an imperial Frankenstein, Plato's perennial philosopher tyrant. *It is not your shiny institutions but the law of God set before you that is*

---

[6] Mead, Margaret, and James Baldwin. *A Rap on Race*. Vintage Books, 1971, p. 134.; You are melted down by propagandists into "implements of bronze and iron" (Genesis 4:22) by "Jubal…the father of all those who play the lyre and flute;" by the "troubadours, the bards that go from town to town, building the stories of the cities." In this case, instruments of bronze and iron that connote war and violence.; Tarazi, Paul Nadim. "Music and War." *The Bible as Literature - Tarazi Tuesdays*, 22 Aug. 2023, tbal.transistor.fm/episodes/music-and-war.

[7] Before British colonization, Palestinians coexisted as villagers, townspeople, and Bedouins. This is not to be equated with the colonial Melting Pot, which imposes philosophical "equality" and "integration." The Palestinians coexisted in the Pauline sense, each as they were found in the palm of God's hand. This may be best reflected in the sublime novelty and intricacy of Palestinian embroidery and dress of each village and town, now erased.; Wikipedia contributors. "Palestinian Traditional Costumes." *Wikipedia*, June 2023, en.wikipedia.org/wiki/Palestinian_traditional_costumes#CITEREFNeedler1949p._87.

exceptional. In all things, the only differentiator is the absence or presence of this law, which undermines all human systems, dynasties, and beliefs to safeguard transient life in the wilderness.

The Tribal Patriarch

In his seminal work, *The Rise of Scripture*, Father Paul Tarazi explains how the biblical writers extended the line of scriptural critique from the Greeks onto the Roman Empire, the chief institutional inheritors of ancient Hellenism. Against Roman tyranny, these writers employed the metaphor of *shepherdism*: In observation of the Syrian desert, the biblical authors perceived the role of the shepherd as our natural human state. Human beings are not exceptional. We are, however, accountable to care for *all* life that dwells in our locality. It follows for Scripture that the families of the earth included the other land mammals. Unlike the residents of an artificial city, a shepherd cares for his flock in and among the families of the earth in subsistence living near a natural oasis. Where a family is created by God, a city is built by man. Where a child is born from a mother's womb, a statue is fashioned by man. Where a king or leader is chosen by man, a shepherd is assigned by God.

A shepherd roams freely in the wilderness, away from the artificial center, outside the institutional boundaries of king and city. His sheep find life with him through obedience to his voice. The scriptural writers co-opt this voice for the recitation of God's law:

Dark Sayings

"Then I will set over them one shepherd, my slave David, and he will feed them; he will feed them himself and be their shepherd." (Ezekiel 34:23)

It is tempting for Hellenized thinkers to extract a morality from this contrast between king and shepherd. What are the good attributes of a shepherd? Should we be meek, like the simple shepherds? How can we become good shepherds? Listen carefully to the blasphemy in your question. You want to become a "good shepherd?" (John 10:11) A shepherd is not "good" because he embodies a set of values or ethical norms, human or scriptural. *It is not the shepherd but the law of God set before him that is exceptional.* As Jesus said, and it bears constant repeating:

"Why do you call me good? No one is good except God alone." (Mark 10:18)

The law of God set before you—his written commands without human imagination or emotionalism—*this* law is good. This law undermines and overrides all institutional norms to safeguard life in the wilderness, away from the artificial center, free from conflict, shame, condescension, cruelty, and abuse. "For freedom," Paul proclaims, "Christ has set us free." (Galatians 5:1)

During Rome's post-Republic era, the Pauline school found a strategic opportunity for the biblical message in the local distribution of divine power. Having declared

The Refugee Church

himself the "Son of God,"[8] Augustus, son of Julias[9] Caesar, became Roman society's organizing premise.

The execution of every need depended on situational power, as it pertained to Caesar's divine authority. By law, the Roman family was organized *patria potestas*, by the power of a father, and Caesar, *pater patriae*,[10] stood out as the father of fathers. A Roman father exercised authority over his children, their descendants, and their property. For those living in his household, *his locality*, the father functioned *as* Caesar *under Caesar, his* father. Remember that a Roman household was no nuclear family but more akin to a small neighborhood. Since the day-to-day necessities of Roman life centered around the father's situational power, the *paterfamilias* emerged as a functionary of Caesar's divine power for the needs

---

[8] Syme, Ronald. *The Roman Revolution.* Oxford, 1939, pp. 112-13.

[9] In his lifetime, Julias allowed an effigy of himself to be carried in procession with the other gods and had a second installed in the shrine of Romulus. He also patterned his residence on Palatine Hill after temple architecture, posing as a god among men under the title "Jupiter Julias," following the example of his chosen "prototype," Alexander the "great."; Robinson, Cyril. *A History of the Roman Republic.* 1932, pp. 419-420.

[10] George Washington was annointed the same, inscribed in stone, coin, and bust.; Childs Gallery. "Patriae Pater (Father of His Country) (George Washington) (the Porthole Portrait) | Childs Gallery." Childs Gallery, 28 Aug. 2018, childsgallery.com /work/patriae-pater-father-of-his-country-george-washington-the-porthole-portrait.; Hind, C. Lewis. Augustus Saint-Gaudens, by C. Lewis Hind. 1908, p. 92.; "Eulogy on George Washington Delivered in St. Peter's Church, Baltimore, February 22, 1800, by John Carroll, First Bishop and Archbishop of Baltimore" HathiTrust, 1931, babel.hathitrust.org/cgi/pt?id=wu.89077174795&seq=7, p. 21.

of the local Roman *familia*. In all private matters, he embodied the functional will of the person of Caesar, with full authority to execute Caesar's judgment, including capital punishment.[11]

This then became the genius of the New Testament writers: Using the function *paterfamilias*, the biblical authors replaced Caesar, Rome's *pater patriae*, with the God of Abraham. Just as *Elohim* (the plural of *Eloah*) became the face of God overwriting all gods in the ancient world, through the letters of St. Paul and the gospels, in the mind of a baptized Roman citizen, *Elohim* became the face of Caesar to the people of Rome.

Targeting Caesar's divine authority as a single point of failure, the New Testament emasculated Caesar by transforming the Roman patrician into a functionary of Jesus Christ. What once pertained to Caesar now pertained to God vis-à-vis the station of the *paterfamilias*. Tarazi explains:

> *"Roman society was fundamentally tribal, the basic societal unit being not so much the city but the "household" whose head was the "father" (Latin paterfamilias). The paterfamilias had as full and incontrovertible authority as the 'ab of Bedouin shepherd society. In the Old Testament, the authors frontally attacked the Greeks and offered them a society patterned after shepherdism. In the New Testament, the strategy changed. It opted for "taming," "harnessing" the opponent by using the Roman traditions against the imperial*

---

[11] This parallels a shepherd's purview over the life of an individual sheep.; Rodriguez, Emily, and Gaurav Shukla. "Roman Law." *Encyclopedia Britannica*, 2016, www.britannica.com/topic/patria-potestas.

The Refugee Church

power, which was the real nemesis of the power of God and his anointed. The Pauline school used the Roman household as the ekklēsia (kat' oikon ekklēsia; house church), the scriptural qahal that is summoned by the father's voice according to his pleasure."[12]

The Roman family, a tribal unit organized around the authority of its patriarch, no longer yielded to the institutional norms of Rome, but to the authority of God the Father, through the teaching of Jesus Christ. Terrifying and dangerous, indeed. The Roman family, under its patriarch,[13] became a beachhead for the scroll of God's teaching in the Empire, right under Caesar's Hellenized nose.[14]

---

[12] Tarazi, Paul Nadim. *The Rise of Scripture*. OCABS Press, 2017, p. 336.

[13] Or **matriarch**/*materfamilias*. See Lydia, Acts 16:14-15,40. The sole concern of the biblical text is functional authority for the sake of its enforcement, to which **gender is irrelevant.** Lydia Lithos (or Petri) is a dense, black basaltic rock found along the coastline of ancient Lydia in the Ionia region of Asia Minor used by merchants to test the purity of gold. Lydia, *materfamilias*, "a seller of purple fabrics, a worshiper of God, was listening; and the Lord opened her heart to respond to the things spoken by Paul. And when she and her household had been baptized," she became useful to God as his *locum tenens*, to bring about (to confirm, test, discern) the truth from the lie. The text of Acts, in its construction of Lydia's character, possibly conceived of her as a black woman.; "Λυδία Λίθος - Η Πέτρα Τής Αλήθειας." Κοσμήματα Σταύρου Χαλάνδρι, kosmimata-stavrou.gr/blog/ λυδία-λίθος-η-πέτρα-τής-αλήθειας.

[14] Biblical Hebrew is the "concocted" Semitic language of Scripture, part and parcel of the content of God's *debarim* to his people against Hellenism and Hellenistic imperialism. It is integral to the content of God's teaching, written to set his people free—*in their minds*—from the tyranny of Alexander the "great" and, later, in the storyline of the New Testament, the Caesars.; Ibid., 475.

Dark Sayings

In God's Hands

Like a baptized Roman household, my childhood community—the product of civil war, broken relationships, conflict, and estrangement—found life in the palm of God's hand, hiding in plain sight from the institutional center. This made life possible for me as a child and allowed me to grow up in relative peace and safety. While others fell prey to the culture now spiraling around us, I caught a glimpse of the hospitality, fraternity, and deep conviction of duty characteristic of the best version of the people of the Middle East. For this, I live each day in submission, offering priestly ministry to God in thanksgiving for my parents, my mother's parents, and my aunts and uncles, who all contributed to that homeland of my heart's desire, now gone. At a time when the world around me is turning to ash and dung from the worship of money, my memory of that place—recreated inside me and repurposed by the seed of the gospel—sustains me.

If anything was good and beautiful about our refugee church, it came not from us but from the work of a few teachers forgotten generations ago, who preached the gospel of Jesus Christ to the nomadic peoples of the Middle East. They are gone, and now we are gone, but the seed of Scripture remains:

> *"As for man, his days are like grass; Like a flower of the field, so he flourishes. When the wind has passed over it, it is no more, and its place no longer knows about it. But the mercy of the Lord is from everlasting to everlasting for those who fear him, and his justice to the children's children, to*

The Refugee Church

those who keep his covenant and remember his precepts, so as to do them." (Psalm 103:15–18)

All things come to an end, but the words of God do not come to an end. Everything dies, but not everything has the power to sustain life. Our church life followed the pattern of subsistence living in the Syrian wilderness, centered on hearing the gospel (however meager our education at the time) and our weekly participation in the liturgy. We were a nomadic, patriarchal, Bedouin-styled, anti-institutional church [15] with no homeland, sense of belonging, or connection to an ideological center.

ST. PAUL DID NOT BUILD or establish churches. He fell upon existing families, like mine, communities in physical proximity to him along the road, and shared the gospel with their patriarch. [16] Hence his literary-

---

[15] In Palestinian villages, the *ḥamūla* (extended family groups, from *ḥamala*, to carry, literally, a "female carrier," in Hebrew, *ḥamal*, Ezekiel 16:5, to bear with) ensured social stability through a patronymic system of moral obligations to each other under the powerful guidance of the patriarch. Land tenure was shared under *mushaʻa* communal practice.; Al-Salim, Farid. "Landed Property and Elite Conflict in Ottoman Tulkarm." *Center for Palestine Studies, Columbia University*, Mar. 2017, pp. 65–80. palestine.mei.columbia.edu/jerusalem-quarterly-2/2017/3/30/issue-47, p. 69.

[16] In any tribal setting, the introduction of the gospel forces a pivotal decision. In ancient Rome, the dilemma was a choice between familial allegiance and devotion to the teaching of Jesus. Most often, in the person of the patrician, Romans chose their family, leading to the persecution and death of those spreading the seed of the gospel. In the rare case where a patrician yielded to

honorific title, "Tentmaker." (Acts 18:13) Through the *paterfamilias*, Paul transformed the pre-existing Roman household into the biblical Tent of Meeting.[17] From the Apostle Paul's Tent, wandering in the wilderness of my heart's desire, I preach to you the same gospel at work against me for the sake of the generation yet unborn:

> *"Shall one who hates justice rule? And will you condemn the righteous mighty One, who says to a king, 'Worthless one,' to nobles, 'Wicked ones'; Who shows no partiality to princes nor regards the rich above the poor, for they all are the work of his hands. In a moment, they die, and at midnight, people are shaken and pass away, and the mighty are taken away without a hand. For his eyes are upon the ways of a man, and he sees all his steps. There is no darkness or deep shadow where the workers of iniquity may hide themselves. For he does not need to consider a man further, that he should go before God in judgment. He breaks in pieces mighty men without inquiry and sets others in their place. Therefore, he knows their works, and he overthrows them in the night, and they are crushed. He strikes them like the wicked in a public*

Paul's instruction, the entire family (household) was baptized. However, a third option emerges in modern America: loyalty to oneself. In this context, few prioritize family. Instead, the allure of individualism prevails. As such, the Pauline household is technically impossible in America, where the teacher, the teaching, and the familial hierarchy are all dismissed. "What the [American] system does to the subjugated is to destroy his sense of reality. It destroys, for example, his father's authority over him. His father can no longer tell him anything because his past has disappeared."; Baldwin, James. *The Price of the Ticket: Collected Nonfiction: 1948–1985*. Beacon Press, 2021, p. 408.

[17] Syro-Arabian shepherdism and Roman tribalism are part and parcel of the content of Scripture.

The Refugee Church

*place because they turned aside from following him, and had no regard for any of his ways; so that they caused the cry of the poor to come to him, and that he might hear the cry of the afflicted—When he **yashqit** ("keeps quiet"), who then can condemn? And when he hides his face, who then can behold him, that is, in regard to both nation and man?—So that godless men would not rule nor be snares of the people. (Job 34:17–30)*

And so:

*"You lords **paréchesthe** (Greek, "provide," Hebrew, **shaqat**, "give peace, keep the peace," Arabic, **saqaṭa**, "fall, lose worth, decline, collapse") to your slaves righteousness and equality, knowing that you have a Lord in heaven." (Colossians 4:1)[18]*

---

[18] In the example from Job, the word *yashqit*, a form of the verb *shaqat*, is rendered as *paréchesthe* in the Septuagint Greek. Paul may not be referring to Job, but the functionality of the word in Scripture and its Semitic/Arabic cognate add texture to our hearing of the verse. In your station as a lord, the moment you submit to *the* Lord in the heavens as Jesus did to his Father, making the commandment "judge not" (Matthew 7:1) functional in the minds of those in your charge, *you will be judged* (against Paul's admonition in 1 Corinthians 4:5) *before* the time. Anything of you or by you must fall and collapse in shame so that only the text of the gospel remains until the Lord comes. The *peace* (Hebrew, *shalom*, Arabic, *salam*) bestowed in Colossians 1:2 and provided (made functional) by a lord in 4:1, comes only through total submission (Arabic, *aslama*) to God.

*"Here further up the mountain slope
Than there was ever any hope,
My father built, enclosed a spring,
Strung chains of wall round everything,
Subdued the growth of earth to grass,
And brought our various lives to pass.
A dozen girls and boys we were.
The mountain seemed to like the stir,
And made of us a little while-
With always something in her smile.
Today she wouldn't know our name.
(No girl's, of course, has stayed the same.)
The mountain pushed us off her knees.
And now her lap is full of trees."*

—*Robert Frost, The Birthplace*

The Pearl of Great Price

"Again, the kingdom of heaven is like a merchant seeking fine pearls, and upon finding one pearl of great value, he went and sold everything that he had and bought it." (Matthew 13:45-46)

There is an ancient practice in human society common to all cultures. For as long as there have been painters, chefs, carpenters, or practitioners of any kind, humans have understood that the best way to learn a master's skill is to repeat it. This principle may be a curiosity lost on the sensibilities of modern education, but in Scripture, it is foundational. As a young man, from the first moment I heard my spiritual father[19] preach the gospel, the dignity and honor conveyed by his words made an indelible impression on me. I knew I wanted the same for myself. Perhaps because of my cultural roots, I immediately understood that repetition was the best way to achieve this. So, I began a lifelong journey to repeat the master's words.

To my ears, his teaching was the Pearl of Great Price, a treasure of pure gold that caused the oppressive frailty of individualism, consumerism, and militarism to evaporate around me. If this person's words could have such an impact on me, I knew that I was responsible for spreading them. Fueled by a sense of duty, I had to return home with his message and share it with

---

[19] I heard and was adopted by a *pater familias* into a new *familia*. We do not find God. We are found: *"But now that you have come to know God, or rather to be known by God, how is it that you turn back again to the weak and worthless elemental things, to which you desire to be enslaved all over again?" (Galatians 4:9)*

The Pearl of Great Price

everyone—friends, family, community, strangers—because there was something about the honor those words embodied. Yes, Scripture is full of drama and bravado to be channeled by the preacher, but it was more than that. Those words were honorable because they penetrated and dignified the parts of my sojourn that were ugly, corrupt, and irredeemable—places deep inside full of darkness and utter ignorance. I knew that this honor, the light of instruction, God's Torah, was not something I wanted only for myself but something I was now responsible for teaching.

In the context of the Torah, when I say "honor," I mean the honor associated with the knowledge of what is written in Scripture. I grew up in an anti-intellectual environment where the people around me were intelligent but unwilling to ask hard questions. Intelligence and depth are not the same thing. Spend twenty minutes in corporate America, and you will understand my point. Or maybe you won't because this is America, where teachers, professors, and clergy in our time have become the sycophants of corporate CEOs and Silicon Valley. Plenty of smart people do not ask hard questions about real topics. People want the weather, sports, politics, ideology, gossip, entertainment—in other words, bullshit. It is like Facebook before there was a Facebook. Any effort to scratch beneath the surface—to explore the underlying sin that now makes public demonstrations of gun violence routine—was and is shunned with ridicule and passive-aggressive comments given to sideline the necessary story of violence, ignorance, and cruelty found in the Bible.

Dark Sayings

Standing in judgment before my teacher, all of these experiences dissipated. Suddenly, I found myself in an environment where I could be taught by a man who not only insisted upon a deeper discussion of Scripture, biblical languages, and culture but also understood that Scripture was the only honorable and useful thing to discuss. Everything else was vain talk—empty and pointless, like gossip. "Great minds," Eleanor Roosevelt famously quipped, "discuss ideas; average minds discuss events; small minds discuss people." To be an adult, a father, and useful was to be as knowledgeable as possible in all things, beginning with Scripture. No one had ever opened the world to me in this way. It was adulthood, in the truest sense: to possess knowledge and wisdom for the sake of the common good.[20]

I would be a liar if I said there was no sin in my desire for honor. Of course, there was. Who in their mid-twenties would not want to be recognized and respected? I wanted a way out of the ignorance of my childhood. It is not that I did not have a wonderful childhood and beautiful parents. Still, I grew up in the anti-intellectual, passive-aggressive Midwest—the land of materialism, complacency, entitlement, comfort, and self-congratulatory American exceptionalism;[21] a world

---

[20] Greek *sympheron* ("common good," literally, "together, carry so as to realize a shared benefit") 1 Corinthians 12:7); For context, see 1 Corinthians 10:24.

[21] "We are not special. We don't live in a special place and not in a special time." Avi Loeb, Frank B. Baird Jr. Professor of Science at Harvard University, explains the Copernican principle's social implications.; Lex Fridman. "Avi Loeb: Aliens, Black Holes, and

The Pearl of Great Price

where angry people take their issues out on each other amid a huge deficit of depth, understanding, and empathy. The gospel cut through all that bullshit to present something of value, and I was all in.

After my ordination, I naively assumed that people would recognize this exceptional value of the Pearl of Great Price, just as I did, and understand the importance of my preaching for the sake of the common good. But boy, was I wrong. Before nurses, doctors, and teachers were absurdly belittled during the Pandemic, I learned the horrible lesson that in the United States, no one understands themselves, their neighbor, or their station in terms of the community. Everyone's attitude is "You do your thing, and I'll do mine." In this society, everyone equates their station with everyone else's. A business professional traveling first class internationally really believes he is equal to or even more important than a young mother traveling coach with children. But he is not. She is raising children for the common good while he is raising money. If you find yourself struggling with this point, I feel sorry for you. Worse, I feel sorry for the unborn generation destined to suffer under the tyranny of your ideology, which is why I am still preaching.

No one today seems to understand that certain stations in life pertain to the common good and are, therefore, more important than others—such as mothers, teachers, nurses, doctors, and civil servants.

---

the Mystery of the Oumuamua | Lex Fridman Podcast #154." *YouTube*, 13 Jan. 2021, www.youtube.com/watch?v=plcc6E-E1uU.

Dark Sayings

Their work benefits all of us. But for those who claim to follow God, the one who preaches Scripture should be held in special regard—not because of the messenger, who is no better than anyone else (according to Scripture, the preacher is *defacto* the biggest hypocrite of all) but because of the exceptional value of the message—the Pearl of Great Price.

Unfortunately, each American's insistence on their own importance is so great that no value is placed on public service of any kind, except for those who carry out violence, because they protect everyone's security and, of course, the right to self-importance. So, from the start, and to my foolish surprise, there was no honor in the American priesthood or in teaching the gospel, even before there were consequences for the content of the message itself. There is no honor in serving the common good because, today, everyone in the United States lives for themselves.[22]

---

[22] Once, a parishioner from the Middle East was so lonely in Minnesota (even Prince, the pride of the Minneapolis art scene, spoke of thriving *de*spite the culture's unbearable loneliness—or perhaps *in* "spite" of it) that he would beg me to visit his family unannounced. "Ya Abouna, I will leave my door unlocked during the week. Please, don't tell me when you are coming. Just walk in and say 'hello.' No appointments, *please*. Just give me some sanity, some humanity, ya Abouna." Whereas the institutionalized, when I mention that there is work to be done, explain at length and in detail the contents of their calendar—*their agenda*—asking for "options" from the priest before concluding that they do not "have" time. The Lord said: *"Let your 'Yes' be 'Yes,' and your 'No' be 'No.' For whatever is more than these is from the evil one." (Matthew 5:37);* Jeffries, Judson L., Shaheen, Fred Mark, et al. *Feel My Big Guitar: Prince and the Sound He Helped Create.* UP of Mississippi, 2023. pp. 57-75.

The Pearl of Great Price

Despite the lack of honor given, my own sense of priestly honor and dignity remained undaunted. As St. Paul teaches, am I pleasing men, or am I pleasing God? So, I persisted in doing all of it—studying, reading, repeating, and teaching Scripture the way my teacher taught it, even before I fully understood the words of Scripture or the teaching. This process continued for decades, and I remained faithful to it despite constant pressure from family, clergy, parishioners, and friends to veer from this path. Thank God in the heavens that I am a stubborn Arab, like my dad; however, with respect to fearlessness in preaching, that comes strictly from the text itself.

The Seed

I want to reiterate something that I have said repeatedly over the years, and that has come true in daily life—something I could not have predicted as a young man in my twenties. If you faithfully repeat the words of Scripture, if you keep repeating them exactly as you are commanded to speak them, if you stay the course, no matter your intentions—even if it begins with sin and a desire for honor or glory on human terms—if you imitate the master's trust and submit to the text, the seed does what the seed does. You have no control over the seed, for better or for worse.

To preach according to Scripture, you must not say what you think, what you want to say, what the parish council wants to hear, what will please the people, what will grow the parish, what will satisfy the church hierarchy, what is politically expedient, what fits with the culture in which you minister, what will please your

Dark Sayings

family or friends, or what will make you popular. Instead, you must stick to what you are commanded to preach in the story, with no regard for the reaction of others or your audience. You must lean into the pain of the gospel and, ultimately, the pain of everyday life—unafraid to go to those sinful and scary places where it hurts the most, which is where the story takes you if you are paying attention. You must take seriously the admonition that Paul lays out in Galatians—that you are not standing on the sacred step to please men but to please God. If you are faithful to that teaching, then the seed does what the seed does.

For whatever reason, I have always had an attitude of standing on the outside of arguments and asking questions—not just on the topic of religion. It is interesting because I am naturally a people pleaser. In any case, perhaps because of my dad's critical voice, God put me on the city's outskirts with John the Baptist, willing to go against the grain despite my natural tendency towards pleasing others. Even as a preteen, I was deeply convinced that if something is correct, it does not matter what people think—it must be said. I am not always faithful to this principle in other areas of life, but when it comes to preaching, I tow this line to a fault.

The seed is embryonic. It has its own internal program, not the preacher's words or human theology. It is the biblical text, the divine word inscribed in the Book of Life. If you submit to it as such, you are repeating something written down by the finger of God himself, not by the church. These are the words of God, and if you do not submit to them as such, you are

The Pearl of Great Price

worshiping yourself on Sunday. In that case, you should put this book down and go watch Netflix.

If you worship the God of Abraham, the Scriptural God, you must accept that the church did not write Scripture. It is the Word of God, not the word of his children. On this point, there is no debate. Either you are a secular humanist justifying your institutional identity, which makes you like the average neopagan of this age, or you believe in the Scriptural God, and it is not your Bible. If you trust in this God, Elohim, you must accept that it is his seed, not yours. As I said, his seed does what he wants it to do—it is a program with its own agenda.

After twenty years of preaching against the grain under the authority of my spiritual father, I can tell you that this seed operates within and against the church institution, families, and the human heart. Most importantly, it operates *against me*. This happens only in the rare case when it is not carefully, attentively, and faithfully swept under the rug by those desperate to grow their church into a thriving and dynamic community so that one day they can build a bigger building with a trust fund in their name.

At this juncture, it is important to note that the Parable of the Sower, as told in Matthew and Mark, was not written in, about, or for the modern Midwest. It was set in first-century Palestine in the story of the Bible, where *God* arranged the land.

The Sower went out to sow his seed without the aid of modern farming tools or practices such as tractors or tilling. There were no even or well-groomed rows

Dark Sayings

spanning acres of level terrain. The ground varied in its composition, with some areas being rocky or thorny. Still, the seed remained consistent in its operation. Again, the point of the parable is not the soil but the consistency and persistence of the seed. If the seed, which does only one thing, fails to take root in one location, it will do so in another. The soil has no agency in this process. We do not like to hear that message because we want control, but we have none. Our only hope is to submit to the words of the parable—the content of the seed—which confronts us with our own powerlessness and corruption. In first-century Palestine, there was no way to prepare the countryside for sowing. The implication of the parable is that those hearing the instruction must either submit to the words of Jesus (or Moses) and find life or reject them and perish:

> *"I call heaven and earth to witness against you today, that I have placed before you life and death, the blessing and the curse. So choose life in order that you may live, you and your descendants, by loving the Lord your God, by obeying his voice, and by holding close to him; for this is your life and the length of your days, so that you may live in the land which the Lord swore to your fathers, to Abraham, Isaac, and Jacob, to give them." (Deuteronomy 30:19-20)*

When you plant the seed, the soil will react in different but ultimately *irrelevant* ways. People are greedy, lazy, entitled, arrogant, ensnared by the victim mentality, preoccupied, and, in the end, do not want to be bothered. Mostly, we do not want to face the emptiness, sin, cruelty, or pain the seed exposes because we do not want to face the truth about ourselves. Like the soil, even

The Pearl of Great Price

the preacher has no agency except to spread the seed that condemns him.

Only the seed, the purview, not of Jesus, but of Elohim, has agency, containing everything it needs to make a tree or a plant. Not the soil, not even the Sower, but the seed contains the value assigned by God. When the soil reacts negatively in Mark, Jesus moves on quickly to the next potential disciple. In other words, it does not matter what people think. The current crop is dying on the vine, and winter is coming. The urgency is in the spreading of the seed.

KEEP PREACHING!

A Church History Lesson

Each year, January marks the anniversary of the bloody Nika riots, a series of violent civil disturbances in Constantinople in 532 AD against the oppressive rule of Emperor Justinian. The underlying reasons for the riots were excessive taxation, government corruption, and the harsh treatment of debtors. The immediate cause was Justinian's botched handling and eventual ruthless execution of two charioteers. Refusing to step down from power, Justinian crushed the protests using professional Byzantine soldiers and his personal Viking guards, systematically executing 30,000 people. [23] In the aftermath of the massacre, the emperor consolidated his power, ordering the murder of a popular Roman consul, Hypatius,[24] stripping his family of land and title, even though Justinian knew Hypatius was not behind the revolt. Eighteen senators were similarly banished. With a total population of only 300,000,[25] no family living in the "City of the Virgin" was untouched by Justinian's brutality. After the Nika massacre, Constantinople settled into a dreadful silence. No one would ever again challenge Justinian's power.

The Nika massacre marked a turning point in Justinian's reign. Within one month of Constantinople's

---

[23] Stephenson, Paul. *Constantine: Roman Emperor, Christian Victor*. Abrams, 2010, p. 275.

[24] Treadgold, Warren T. *A History of the Byzantine State and Society*. Stanford UP, 1997, p. 181.

[25] Boeck, Elena N. *The Bronze Horseman of Justinian in Constantinople: The Cross-Cultural Biography of a Mediterranean Monument*. Cambridge UP, 2021, p. 39.

A Church History Lesson

devastation by fire, construction of a new cathedral was already underway, evidence that Justinian had collaborated with architects on a new design for the eastern capital as early as 527 AD. Moved by personal ambition and a desire to establish a Roman legacy in the East, Justinian is quoted by sources as wanting to "outdo Solomon" in the construction of a new temple.[26]

At the time, the Church of St. Polyeuktos, which had survived the riots, was the largest temple in Constantinople. Built by Anicia Juliana, it represented a threat to Justinian's imperial and divine legitimacy.[27] Anicia was the daughter of the Roman emperor Olybrios and the great-granddaughter of the emperor Theodosios II. Her great-grandmother, Empress Aelia,[28] is a saint in the Orthodox church. To make matters worse for Justinian, the first Hagia Sophia, built by Aelia's great-grandfather more than a century earlier, was among several churches destroyed in the riots. If anyone else could legitimately replace Justinian (even after a terrifying massacre), it was Anicia.

With ample wealth accumulated from his oppressive tax schemes, Justinian initiated a five-year project to build the infamous "Hagia Sofia," now restored as a Mosque in modern-day Türkiye. Justinian was fifty years old when he commissioned the project. He wanted to live long enough to see his mosaic installed in the

---

[26] Barker, John W. *Justinian and the Later Roman Empire*. Univ of Wisconsin Press, 1966, p. 183.
[27] Bell, Peter N. *Social Conflict in the Age of Justinian: Its Nature, Management, and Mediation*. Oxford UP, 2013 pp. 323-324.
[28] Wikipedia contributors. "Anicia Juliana." *Wikipedia*, Apr. 2023, en.wikipedia.org/wiki/Anicia_Juliana.

Dark Sayings

cathedral's entryway, so he gave his builders an unlimited budget under an aggressive deadline. Ten-thousand laborers worked daily to complete the project, taxing precious raw materials from all over the empire, including 320,000 pounds of gold.[29] The project was completed in five years, ten months, and four days. At a procession during the cathedral's first liturgy, again, Justinian is reported to have said, "Solomon, I have outdone you."[30]

It's an interesting attribution. The biblical Solomon, too, murdered or exiled anyone who threatened his power and levied a tax to build a temple that would consolidate his authority at a high cost of human labor. Unlike Justinian, Solomon's project took seven years; in biblical terms, less merciful than five. In Justinian's eyes, the length of Solomon's project was probably seen as a sign of weakness. This author does not accuse Justinian of hearing, let alone understanding, Scripture.

Reflecting on the Hamline University scandal in a homily,[31] I noted that a teacher does not share information to offend or pacify feelings. Teachers impart whatever they learn; they share whatever they

---

[29] Flash Point History. "History of Byzantium - Vol 3 - Nika Riots / Vandal War / Hagia Sophia." *YouTube*, 17 May 2022, www.youtube.com/watch?v=VYvc71OPzuo.

[30] Ibid.

[31] Patel, Vimal. "A Hamline Adjunct Showed a Painting of the Prophet Muhammad. She Lost Her Job." *The New York Times*, 20 June 2023, www.nytimes.com/2023/01/ 08/us/hamline-university-islam-prophet-muhammad.html.

A Church History Lesson

discover and pass it on—be it historical, natural, or, if it concerns faith, scriptural.

Unfortunately for Hamline's eager censors and their Muslim students, it remains a fact that there are paintings of the prophet Mohammed. Albeit embarrassing for Christians, it is also a fact that emperor Justinian was a murderer, condemned by Scripture, which ridicules the sons of Cain, who look to secure their legacy in temples of stone. How we feel about these facts has no bearing on their validity, significance, or the urgency with which we must teach them. The alternative is to endure endless church planning meetings about "building" or "growing" something for God's glory when what we want, in truth, is our mosaic plastered next to Justinian's picture above the cathedral entrance.

Bow or Walk Away

Theologians love to philosophize about the darkness in the world because, like politicians, they fancy the work of their own hands as a city of light set upon a hill. They see themselves as the administrators of light in a world gone astray. Nothing could be further from the story of the Bible, which shines its powerful light to expose the darkness in each of us, unimpeded by our crafty designs on self-importance.

When we are personally touched by the pain-filled light of Scripture, we find ourselves grappling with something we refuse to see—a darkness that fills everything we say, do, create, maintain and defend.

In Scripture, the latter is represented by the Temple in Jerusalem. However, for the average person who likes to complain about the hypocrisy of religion or the local priest, ask yourself, how much do you spend on your house, your car, your family, your entertainment, or your savings vs. the poor? How are your household, your family, or your friends any different than the Temple in the Bible or any other institution? To the extent that any of these draw a line between you and the beggar, they're not.

At this point, a flood of justifications and rationalizations enter your mind. If this were a sermon, you might take the message personally and lash out in some way. Why? Not because you love money and security, per se, or because you are sick of hearing the same message. You are, of course, but this is not the main issue. The real concern is: One, you want to be right with God, or at least, you want to be right in

Bow or Walk Away

general, and two, the part of you that is honest knows that you are going to keep your house, buy the things that you want to buy, and have no plans to invite a beggar to sleep in your spare room.

So, you are stuck. You either must lie to yourself about the words of Scripture or accept your place among the brood of vipers hailed by John the Baptist in Luke 3. Another option, of course, is to complain that the Bible does not make sense—but this also is a lie. It does make sense, you just don't like what it says because the truth is, you can't do it. Few of us can—except the rare birds who give their life for the teaching, which presently excludes all of us. In the end, if you are an honest person, you can either bow down to Scripture, confess your sins, and learn from them, or you can walk away feeling justified.

The choice, as they say, is yours.

Why I Do Not Vote

(Homily, Sunday, April 30, 2023)

In the name of the Father and of the Son of the Holy Spirit. Amen.

Christ is Risen!

You know, I said to Richard on the eve of Pascha that, as a priest, I could stop the Holy Week services on Great Friday or the Vesperal Liturgy on Saturday morning. Unfortunately, the Paschal service, in the way that it is celebrated, does not capture what Scripture is saying. In the biblical story, you are not presented with your

Dark Sayings

victory; instead, you are confronted with the empty tomb and the coming Judgment.

The way that we celebrate Pascha—steeped in the imperial pageantry of the Roman Empire—one gets the impression that St. Paul did not write his first letter to the Corinthians, or at least, one gets the impression that we missed the memo. In principle, this problem can be salvaged in the preaching. For years, I have tried to emphasize that the Paschal candle, carried so gracefully today for us by Cecelia (and last week by Josie), is affixed with a cross. Still, people skip the forty days of Lent, barely show up for Holy Week, and then explain wistfully, "You see, Father, you can't separate the two; you can't separate the joy from the suffering."

People speak this way out of cowardice. They are afraid of pain, and they cannot face the truth about themselves, about life, their place in it, and what comes next. They want Jesus to come down from the Cross. That is why the Orthodox love Joseph of Arimathea. They love nice rich guys who make the pain go away.

Standing before the empty tomb of the scriptural Pascha, the view you are presented with in the story is the vanity of the situation in which you now find yourself.

According to the story, the hope of the Resurrection is not running around saying, yay, we win because we get to live forever. "Christ is risen," the way *we* shout it, is not the good news of the Bible. According to the story, the good news is the harsh and, yes, terrible judgment of God's instruction.

Bow or Walk Away

It is God's judgment that pierces the vanity of the grave. Christ is raised in power and coming in judgment, but this is not how we Orthodox speak. This is not how our services function for us, and after more than twenty years of ministry, it is very painful for me as an Orthodox priest.

Over the years, I have explained in many and various ways that because of Scripture, I do not believe in anything. I know that this terrifies people.

I do not believe[32] in community.
I do not believe in family.
I do not believe in relationships.

I believe only in the Scriptural God.[33]

---

[32] In Greek *pistis* means trust. To believe, in Scripture, is to place one's trust.

[33] Oliver Anthony, explaining peace (*shalom/salam*) through submission (*aslama*) to God: "I'd been in church growing up, and I had been exposed to all that, but I'd found a lot of theatrics and a lot of politics in church and in religion when I was younger, and so it just immediately turned me off to it…I mean, I've been reading [Scripture] here and there off and on…I just had a breakdown moment. I just felt hopeless like almost the way a child feels hopeless…like a like a four-year-old that can't find his parents (Matthew 19:14) …I quit worrying about me and started worrying about what it is that I'm supposed to do. You know, like it talks in the Bible about being a servant and, you know, giving up I guess my desire and my will and whatever it is that I want to do…it's about trying to use what I have as a tool versus doing what I can in the moment to give myself whatever satisfaction that it is I'm trying to get…it's about trying to let go of your ego, and, I mean, people pursue that mentality without faith. I mean, it's the idea of there

Dark Sayings

I do not believe in ideas.
I do not believe in politics.
I do not believe in the system.

I believe only in the Scriptural God.

I do not believe in a career.
I do not believe in progress.
I do not believe in growth.

I believe only in the Scriptural God and what he demands of me: that everything human—beginning with me—is canceled.

Now, it is disingenuous for me to say this to you because, like all men, I am a liar.

As soon as church is over this morning, I will go to the parking lot and enjoy a comfortable ride home in my Nissan Leaf. I gave my money to Nissan, which means,

---

being something bigger than you. But I think inherently all human beings idolize something. Like it talks in the Bible about false idols. We all have false idols…It's very difficult for a human to be the biggest thing on their hierarchy. There's always something above us, right? Because we're always in pursuit of something bigger than us whatever it is in that moment. And I think for me it was just about taking everything else, all the distractions and all the other things in my life away and just ensuring that at least—and look…we all sin, and we all do stupid things like we're all just people. Nobody's special or righteous. People sometimes act like they're special and righteous, but we're all just the same thing…it's just about trying to make [the God of Scripture]—make that my idol…[make] what it is he wants done on this earth my idol versus anything else. You know, we all serve some master whether we realize it or not. So why not let it be the Master that is above all?"; "The Joe Rogan Experience: #2027 - Oliver Anthony." *Spotify*, open.spotify.com /show/ 4rOoJ6Egrf8K2IrywzwOMk.

on some level, I am not fully canceled. I am not yet baptized. I am not a martyr. I gave of myself to something that does not pertain to the Scriptural God, which means I am still an idolater.

But I will not defend my sin. I will not praise Nissan, and I will not rationalize, justify or weasel my way out from under the condemnation of Matthew 23. I simply confess that I am wrong. I am a hypocrite. I am unrighteous. However, the commandment is righteousness, so I preach it boldly, haughtily, and without apology based on its authority, not mine. Do not follow my example, but by all means, imitate my faith.

Years ago, I placed a sign on the bathroom mirror to tease the altar boys:

"And the Lord was sorry that he had made human beings."
(Genesis 6:6)

Scripture is a critique of the human race. It was not written for us but rather addressed to us, against us, for the sake of God's creation. *We are the problem* in the story. It was not written to fix or reform us but to keep us in check, for our sake, yes, but more importantly, for the well-being of all of God's creation, of which, in the story, we are but an insignificant part. We are the squeaky wheel that keeps messing things up for everyone else in the *toledot* (generations) of the heavens and the earth.

The human being is corrupt. Nobody wants to hear this. People want to hear that God loves us and that everything will be okay in the end. But that is not what Scripture is saying. We are the makers of war, poverty, nuclear bombs, and environmental disasters. Our lust

Dark Sayings

for personal engagement has unleashed the beast of social media entanglement, and A.I. is next.

We are the problem.

God has work for us to do, and he gives us his instruction to keep us in check, but we keep pushing back. In Genesis, he regretted creating us because of our relentless rebellion. Accordingly, his story is written in such a way that every generation is intended to *keep hearing* Scripture. The message of Genesis 6:6 is also the message of the Lukan genealogy and the message of every book in the Bible: *nothing changes* under the sun!

If then, the situation is not reparable, the only hope is the one thing that can push back against human arrogance at every turn at all times and in every place for every generation:

Scripture!

That is why *I do not vote* and why I do not have hope in anything except the word of God! Let me repeat: I do not place my hope in anything except the word of God.

I do not place my hope in people.
I do not place my hope in reform.
I do not place my hope in "rules" or the rule of law.

Burn it all. That is exactly what "Christ is risen" means. Namely, that only one thing stands out: the teaching of Jesus Christ. Now, if that is what you mean when I say, "Christ is risen," please, by all means, proclaim that he is risen! Shout it from the rooftops! Then, I will be at ease as a priest.

Bow or Walk Away

But that is not what people mean. What I hear as a priest is, "yeah, but." There is no "yeah, but." Either everything is under the gospel, or it is not:

"For he must reign until he has put all his enemies under his feet. The last enemy that will be abolished is death." (1 Corinthians 15:25–26)

Either every idol we fashion is smashed under the gospel of Jesus Christ, or it is not. I say, from generation to generation, may it be so!

When you say, "Christ is risen," or when you are willing to risk a response by saying, "Indeed, he is risen," you are proclaiming that Christ *exists*. To say that Christ exists is to say linguistically that he *stands out*, for example, the way that I stand the gospel book up on the altar or the way that something is stood up in general or made to stand out. When something stands out, it functions as a *reference*.

In the prophecy of Isaiah, everything in the land lies flattened out except the Lord so that nothing may serve as a reference but God himself, who comes in power and judgment. This is what the Resurrection means. Nothing stands out but God. So, when we say, "Christ is risen," we profess the teaching of St. Paul that everything is subject to God the Father, under the feet of Jesus Christ.

This is the scriptural word of hope to you in the proclamation of the Resurrection. You are under judgment! As Paul says in Galatians, he does not place his hope in those hearing his letter. Likewise, I have no hope in you or me. I have no hope in philosophy or psychology or medicine or business or science or your stupid insurance policies. I have hope in God the Father, who puts all things in subjection under the feet of his Son, trampling down death by death:

> *"For he has put all things in subjection under his feet. But when he says, 'All things are put in subjection,' it is evident that he is excepted who put all things in subjection to him."*
> *(1 Corinthians 15:27)*

JESUS CHRIST IS MY HOPE through his Father's judgment, which stands out above all things for all time through the content of Scripture. We stand at Pascha as those who stand before the terrible and dread judgment seat of Christ!

At the end of this homily, I will proclaim, "Christ is risen." I challenge each of you to consider your response carefully. Look at the Cross. Look carefully upon the one whom *you* have pierced! May your words not fall to the ground as vain talk!

May the Lord's Pascha—the empty tomb pierced by the judgment of the one whom we pierced—strike fear in our hearts unto repentance, and may Jesus Christ return quickly to vindicate the poor.

To God alone be the glory, the dominion, and the majesty; always now and ever and unto ages of ages. Amen.

Christ is risen!

A Mental Vacancy

For years, in homilies and personal discussions with parishioners, family, and friends — I have explained that there is no such thing as progress. That you can't earn anything. That nothing you have belongs to you. No one owes you anything, and even what you seem to have will be taken away, so give it away now because you owe God and your neighbor a debt you can never repay. That you are not a victim—on the contrary—you are the abuser, and you should not keep tabs when you help others because your life does not belong to you.

I have insisted that Scripture is the Pearl of Great Price. The only treasure of value. It is so precious that any time spent talking about anything else is wasted breath. That is why people are sometimes nervous around me during coffee hour, let alone family gatherings.

In recent years I have directed my parish council not to use words like "progress," "success," "legacy," "build," or "engagement" during meetings or in printed materials and notes. I have doggedly acted out Pharisaism publicly so that with each breath when I preach the judgment forcefully, everyone present is certain that I am a hypocrite so that on the off chance that anyone submits to the biblical commandment, they are absolutely clear that it is the righteous commandment that guides their steps and not my example.

I have ridiculed the abuse, criticism, and disrespect of parents (evangelized by popular culture and Disney children's sitcoms) not because our parents are good (no

A Mental Vacancy

one, according to Jesus, is good) but because, as the Good Book proclaims, whatever we are, we are no better, if not worse, than what came before us. I have ridiculed parents, too, because I am a Pharisee, and my job is to preach Psalm 78, like it or not.

I have dismantled our culture, politics, identity, and ideologies of every kind–and still, people want to say, "I agree with you, Father…" Beloved, in Christ, you can't possibly agree with me.[34] Even I disagree with me.

Only the dead agree with Scripture.

Open the Eyes of Your Mind

(Homily, Sunday, May 28, 2023)

In the name of the Father of the Son and the Holy Spirit. Amen.

Christ is in our midst!

I have passed that moment in life where I have any desire—and you'll laugh when I say this because you may think, Father Marc, you were always this way—but no, I wasn't always this way. I have passed that moment where I will hold back what I have to say because death has taught me that the stakes are too high.

This business of Memorial Day, in Scriptural terms, is bad news. It is bad news that every country on Earth celebrates its military might, but it is especially bad news right now in the United States because this is a country, more so than the Roman Empire, that worships

---

[34] The Bible is a rejection of your premise.

Dark Sayings

violence. I have said it to you in many and various ways, but you are not hearing me and do not believe me.

The tradition of this civilization that there is a separation between civil politics and the military is an illusion—a fiction of the Jeffersonian imagination. It is not true. You think it is so because you are followers of the Hellenism of our age that teaches you to think in ontological categories. What do I mean by this?

You imagine that things differ from each other based on their nature as opposed to how they work. You don't look at how things operate in the world. You don't think or analyze. You are led to believe that there is a fundamental difference between two things because of the words people use to deceive you.

Beloved in Christ, our brother, Officer Jaye, brandishes a sidearm every morning and goes out onto the streets to do his job faithfully. You call him a Police Officer, as though in his necessary duties, a Police Officer is something other, but functionally, he is a soldier, and you worship what he brandishes.

You worship violence because, as the Prophets admonish us, violence brings false security to you. You call it freedom, which is what Paul critiques in Galatians. It is not freedom. It is slavery to the power of death. But you worship this worldly security because it provides food, entertainment, and comfort. That is what you worship in this country, and that is what you celebrate on Memorial Day. You celebrate Pharaoh. You celebrate and revel in it at the foot of Sinai like a rebellious teenager who has forgotten who their true Provider is.

A Mental Vacancy

Brothers and sisters, hear my words because they are the words of the Prophets.

We are the rich man who steps over Lazarus on the way to the Temple; On that day, God will not have mercy on us, even if Lazarus intercedes for us.

When you get excited about the love of violence in this country or make a big deal about saving a parking place for soldiers at the grocery store, but at the same time:

- Complain that too many parking spaces are reserved for the handicapped;
- Shame and ridicule nurses during the Pandemic to the extent that they are afraid to wear the garb of their station in public;
- Humiliate teachers, who have the second most important job in the universe (second only to mothers), forcing them to beg for school supplies on the internet, allowing students to abuse them, making them work second jobs to survive;
- Gossip about Native Americans having a few scraps of land left to them called "reservations;"

You should be terrified of the Scriptural God and his coming Kingdom. Run and hide.

You persecute those who provide the very things that matter in God's eyes: rearing of children, care for the sick, bounty for the disenfranchised, and knowledge for the common good. You ridicule and abuse them.

You mock parents in your television shows and shame nurses, diminishing people who take up what "liberated" Americans refuse to do: clean the feces of the elderly or suffer any inconvenience for the benefit of

Dark Sayings

others, squeezing the life out of civil servants for something slightly better than minimum wage.

You deride people who work in public service jobs because you think they owe you your taxes, and you complain about taxation. I happily give half my money away if it will help the country's poor and those working civil service jobs. Not because I believe in politics or the government (I do not) but because my money belongs to God, not to me.

Remember, I do not vote. This is not my kingdom.

Give it away, for Christ's sake. Haven't you figured out what we stand for at St. Elizabeth's? We do not stand for money. We do not stand for violence. We do not stand for power. We do not stand for victory, politics, or party. We stand before the dread and terrible judgment seat of Jesus Christ.

I used to ride the subway to work every single day in New York City. Let me tell you what the United States was, even twenty-five years ago. A pregnant woman would get on the subway train, and no one would give up their seat for her. That's Thomas Jefferson, and I have to listen to Christians offended by Target's advertising campaign lecture me about how the Founding Fathers believed in the Bible. I call baloney because the fruit of the Founding Fathers is a society where a train full of twenty-somethings will not stand up and give their seat to a pregnant woman. That was twenty-five years ago. So, when you are munching on your barbecue this weekend, don't be fooled by Satan's pageantry.

A Mental Vacancy

Don't be fooled by the worship of violence, and don't fall into the trap of self-righteousness, be it the right-wing book-banning crowd or the left-wing woke cancel mob. Like us, they are all under condemnation:

> *"The fool has said in his heart, there is no God. They are corrupt, they have done abominable works, and there is no one that does good. The Lord looked down from heaven upon the children of men to see if there were any that did understand and seek God. They are all gone aside, they are all together become filthy: there is none that does good, no, not one." (Psalm 14:1-3)*

You have no right to judge a soldier, and at the same time, you have no right to worship the gun. You are baptized. You are illumined. You are a child of the Kingdom. You are canceled. You have no rights.

So, when you celebrate Memorial Day this weekend, do not celebrate your freedom, security, and comfort—these are all political euphemisms for violence and cruelty. Instead, celebrate the gospel. Make the Sign of the Cross, bow your head before your true, invisible Master—he who has no flag—and be respectful and caring to *everyone*.

To the returning soldier, yes, by all means—but especially to teachers and parents—the very ones this society hates. To nurses and janitors. To people who clean toilets and wash dishes. To garbage collectors and repairmen and to the person who serves your coffee. Tip everyone at least 20%. If your server is rude, tip them 25%, "for by this some have entertained angels without knowing it." (Hebrews 13:2)

Dark Sayings

But when your president, who doesn't care about the people of Ukraine (whichever president, whichever party, whichever cable news network), makes a speech about liberty, freedom, and justice, while the people living in this neighborhood can't put $2 together to buy a sandwich at El Burrito Market—remember the prayer of St. John Chrysostom before the gospel:

"Open the eyes of your mind!"

St. Paul is challenging you in Galatians not to worship American freedom, which is slavery to death, because in a few years, Ukraine will be a crater in the ground, just like Syria and a dozen other forgotten places. No one cares about Ukraine but the Scriptural God, who does not bless our wars. This is not an opinion. His blessing of our wars is not written. *It is not written.* It is nowhere to be found in the biblical text. *Thus,* it is written:

> *"Woe to you when all men speak well of you, for their fathers used to treat the false prophets in the same way. But I say to you who hear, love your enemies, do good to those who hate you, bless those who curse you, pray for those who mistreat you. Whoever hits you on the cheek, offer him the other also; and whoever takes away your coat, do not withhold your shirt from him either. Give to everyone who asks of you, and whoever takes away what is yours, do not demand it back. Treat others the same way you want them to treat you." (Luke 6:26-31)*

Do not worship those who wield the power of death. Do not worship your flag. Worship instead the teaching of Jesus Christ, our true freedom, which looks nothing like Rome, the United States, or any power ever upon the face of the Earth:

A Mental Vacancy

"It was for freedom that Christ set us free; therefore, keep standing firm and do not be subject again to a yoke of slavery." (Galatians 5:1)

"For you were called to freedom, brethren; only do not turn your freedom into an opportunity for the flesh but serve one another through love." (Galatians 5:13)

Either we are serious about the teaching of Jesus Christ, or we're just playing around in church, like children wearing costumes on Halloween. In the end, that's up to you. But I can tell you, I'm not here to play dress up.

We have a picture of George Floyd near our front steps. This weekend, please think of all the George Floyds who fought for this country, returned home, and could not find a job.

You Minnesotans imagine that life on the corner of 38th and Chicago differs from life in Fallujah. Which life? Whose life?

For the George Floyds of this country, Memorial Day portends tyranny; In their eyes and God's, the Police Officer on the corner is just another border guard.

Change your mind. Look ahead to the coming Kingdom as your only point of reference. Turn and repent for the sake of the poor.

Christ is in our Midst!

In loving memory of Boulos Ishak Boulos on the eighth anniversary of his death.

Heritage is Not Ancestral

In the story of Genesis, the text presents a recurring biblical dilemma: without God's perpetual intervention, life from one generation to the next is impossible. In science and engineering, numerous terms are used to describe similar mechanisms. In physics and thermodynamics, it is referred to as "external energy input" or "external work." In biological systems, which require food, water, and other resources, it is called "homeostasis." Even artificial intelligence requires external input in order to work correctly—though the analogy is not precise—you get the point. In these examples, external input is necessary to prevent catastrophic failure.

In the literary reality of the Bible, like a plant without light or water or an iPhone sitting on the shelf in 1805, each generation of human beings degrades and fails rapidly, to the extent that without God's intervention, there is no possibility of life. In the most obvious of all biblical examples, God intervenes to make a baby when Abraham's seed fails. As far as the Bible is concerned, nothing helpful is passed down from Adam or Abraham, let alone your grandparents or parents. This also means that you, like your forebears, have nothing valuable of yourself to pass on. Why? Because "your origin and your birth are from the land of the Canaanite; your father was an Amorite and your mother a Hittite." (Ezekiel 16:3)

So, if the heritage that gets us out from under the boot of Herod does not come from your family, and the inheritance in question is not from your line, where is it,

Heritage is Not Ancestral

what is it, where does it come from, and who is its beneficiary?

God Does Not Need Your Bread

(Homily, Sunday, June 4, 2023)

In the name of the Father, and of the Son, and of the Holy Spirit. Amen.

Christ is in our midst!

Years ago, as a seminarian, I served at Father Paul's parish on Long Island. One Sunday, I remember his parishioners posted a signup sheet and asked him to announce that volunteers were "needed" to bake church bread.

We are talking about Father Paul, my spiritual father. The man of Scripture who gave birth to me in the gospel. In his way, out of deference to Christ, he refused to make that announcement. Instead of asking for volunteers, after saying a few words about the Sacrifice of Isaac in Genesis, he held that signup sheet up for all to see and proclaimed, "God does not need your bread."

Today, I ask you to memorize this saying and recite it instead of the Jesus Prayer:

"God does not need your bread."

This is the teaching of Scripture.

People in positions of authority in this country, especially parents, teachers, and clergy—or institutions like Parish Councils and School Boards—often base their relationships and interactions with those in their care on "need." Be it emotional, reputational, or financial need—instead of demanding what duty requires for the sake of those in our care—we baby them for personal or institutional gain. No one has the mettle to tell their children, let alone a parishioner, a friend, a family member, or a student:

"God does not need your bread."

Instead, cowards that we are, we host appreciation banquets and give lengthy speeches congratulating our "amazing" volunteers and "generous" donors, coddling fragile egos so that we can build larger temples. Meanwhile, the prophetic books which smash fragile egos and temples of stone are left unopened on the shelf.

As a young priest, I once attended a parish centennial. People gave endless speeches for more than one hour. They praised everyone's accomplishments and bragged about their church. Yet, in all that time, the name of our Lord Jesus Christ was not mentioned, let alone a single verse from the Bible. There is a reason I do not thank my parishioners:

"And Abraham said, 'My son, God will provide for himself the lamb for a burnt offering.'" (Genesis 22:8)

The first retreat I gave as a priest was at St. Mary's Greek Orthodox Church in Minneapolis. I had barely been a priest for six months. I told the participants two things. First, they should take their copies of Plato and Aristotle and burn them. Second, and without apology, I do not need my children.

There was an uncomfortable silence in the auditorium.

Heritage is Not Ancestral

Twenty years later, I have expanded my statement. I do not need my children. I do not need a choir. I do not need altar servers. I do not require volunteers or sign-up sheets, and I do not need parishioners. Thankfully, there is no uncomfortable silence at St. Elizabeth's because all of you are used to me. Still, it's a puzzling teaching for everyone, humanly speaking.

As my dad used to say, it all boils down to priorities.

If we lack people within the church, essential tasks remain incomplete, donations diminish, and bills go unpaid. However, (like the booklets in my childhood church) I have good news for modern man. According to Scripture, our first priority is not the parish's survival. Our first priority is Scripture, which for the sake of failing relationships in this godless society, is teaching you that God does not need you.

If your relationships are founded on need, they bear no resemblance to love. Instead, they are business contracts driven by greed, self-importance, insecurity, manipulation, and selfishness.

If you need something from your children, you are not a parent.

I am not preaching Scripture in order to change this society. This generation and the next, like our building, is already lost. We do not preach to "build" or "grow" St. Elizabeth's. We preach because we are commanded to preach for the generation yet unborn, from which we can gain nothing!

Dark Sayings

In a recent interview, Bill Maher[35] said something fascinating. He explained that when he reviews candidates to work on his program (supposedly the top students in the country), they all sound the same. Same ideas. Same opinions. Same talking points. He can't find a single independent thinker in the bunch. In other words, this generation is lost. Everyone, beginning with the best and the brightest from your top schools, is drinking the Kool-Aid. As Paul says in Ephesians, wake up!

> *"For my thoughts are not your thoughts, neither are your ways my ways, declares the Lord." (Isaiah 55:8)*

Submit to God's thoughts. Follow God's ways, which are not your ways. Learn what it means to love, which has nothing to do with need. To love is to provide for those in need. Any church that brags about itself is no church. Any school that touts its achievements will damage its students. The priest that needs his people is a false prophet. Any parent that needs their children is just another child.

The Western notion that demonstrating vulnerability is a mark of strength in a leader is an abusive lie. When a senior reveals weakness to a junior, they showcase their needs and thus play the victim:

> *"For every beast of the forest is mine, the cattle on a thousand hills. I know every bird of the mountains, and everything that*

---

[35] CNN. "Bill Maher on Wokeness and Why Having an Older President Isn't a Bad Thing." *YouTube,* 1 Mar. 2023, www.youtube.com/watch?v=Ov0a5dETrgE.

Heritage is Not Ancestral

moves in the field is mine. If I were hungry, I would not tell you, for the world is mine, and all it contains." (Psalm 50:10-12)

There is only *one victim* in Scripture.

Consider these things carefully. Examine your conscience before Scripture. When you are with your spouse, friend, child, parent, family member, or anyone else, refrain from asking yourself what they should do or say for you on your terms or for your benefit.

It is not about you or your relationships. Ultimately, it is not even about St. Elizabeth's or the wider community.

It is about Scripture on *its* terms!

We preach because we are commanded to preach for the generation yet unborn, from which we can gain nothing.

God bless you and keep you always.

Christ is in our midst!

No Security Blankets

When a person experiences cognitive dissonance, that is, when they find themselves in a situation where exposure to conflicting ideas and information becomes too stressful or mentally uncomfortable, their natural inclination is to seek security in the safety of consonance. Humans naturally avoid, discredit, belittle, and delegitimize the ideas or people that cause them to experience dissonance.

Today's most common reaction to natural dissonance, especially given the avalanche of information overload, is to bury one's head in the fantasy of suburban bliss. The rise in random acts of public violence is making this much harder, but the white picket fence crowd still manages to hold on to its illusions.

Whether one buries their head in the sand to find peace or seeks out new beliefs or ideas that fit nicely with their own—when you reject dissonance, you seek to place your trust in something comforting: a person or a group of people that looks and sounds like you. You trust those who reflect your values and attitudes—whatever makes you feel safe and secure. You know exactly what we call that in Scripture. You know what they are and what happens to those who trust in them.

On the other hand, Scripture itself is divine dissonance. God challenges you to go against the grain of human thought by trusting his words, knowing full well you have no control over what comes out of his mouth. He will not say what you want, nor will his words or actions reflect your values or attitudes. He will often say exactly what you do not want to hear as if he knows

No Security Blankets

how to betray and embarrass you personally. Pretty cool for a book written by people who did not know you and were not thinking about you and could not possibly have conceived of the modern world when they wrote it.

Scripture liberates you from the fantasy of suburban bliss where Herod's boot is firmly planted on your neck. It challenges you to unplug yourself from the Matrix and accept life in the wilderness, out of your control, but in the palm of God's hand.

The Voice of the Shepherd

(Homily, Sunday, June 11, 2023)

In the name of the Father, and of the Son, and of the Holy Spirit. Amen.

Christ is in our midst!

I was reflecting yesterday on the term "reference" with respect to this morning's gospel and how it relates to the Lord's admonition regarding family:

"Therefore whoever confesses me before men, him I will also confess before my Father who is in heaven. But whoever denies me before men, him I will also deny before my Father who is in heaven. He who loves father or mother more than me is not worthy of me. And he who loves son or daughter more than me is not worthy of me." (Matthew 10:32-33, 37)

Family is an interesting problem in Scripture because, like every association in life, it has its own reference. When I use the term "reference," I refer to the underlying premise, framework, or context that serves

Dark Sayings

as our foundation for comprehending, thinking, assessing, communicating, relating, and behaving in the world. Our reference is our judge.

For years, I have ridiculed the American saying, "family first." I know no one hears or understands what I mean by this criticism or why I am preaching it. I will explain this morning exactly how no one hears me, not only as a priest but as a family member and a corporate professional.

For years, I have noticed a recurring pattern where people come forward to help, advise, or "coach" me using their "reference" as a premise. In almost all these interactions, I find myself sinking into my chair. I sometimes even feel a sense of dread because I know what comes next as a teacher—an irreconcilable and systematic denial of my premise.

There has never been advice given me by a parishioner, a point raised in my professional life by a member of my staff, nor a comment made by anyone in my family that has not rejected my reference—a denial of the premise of the gospel.

Whether it is mundane or something as significant as the Parish Council's obsession with the things we "build," I am alone concerning the gospel.

Just last year, I had a conversation with a colleague who had been struggling with what I was teaching the team. Everyone, including this person, understood what I was asking. They did not like it and did not want to do it because it was difficult.

No Security Blankets

So, I got a lecture about "meeting people where they are." That is a TikTok euphemism for: "I do not like what you say; it is too hard. You need to lower the bar because what you say makes me uncomfortable."

People are neither stupid nor delicate. Everyone can be pushed and is worthy of the challenge. People will always surprise you if you are willing to check your ego at the door. But that takes courage, something in short supply these days.

Instead, we are forced to endure lessons about fragility and safe spaces from those who respect neither themselves nor their neighbors—people who want to lower the bar and bring everyone down to their level, *where nothing happens.*

This, incidentally, is the problem Jesus has with tribe and family. They do not like the words that come out of his mouth. They do not want to hear them. They want to control his lips. They want to bring God down to their level.

Unfortunately for them, the Lord Jesus says what he says exactly as it is written. That is why Scripture is incompatible with theology, family, and institution. God speaks what he speaks. In this sense, from the perspective of your reference, he is unsafe and untrustworthy.

A foolish parent consistently tells their child what the child wants to hear. If you are a wise parent, your child cannot trust the next words from your mouth. It is counterintuitive, so let me repeat. If you are wise, your child has no control over what comes out of your mouth.

Dark Sayings

You are the reference. That is how wisdom works. That is how judgment works. That is how Scripture works.

When someone comes to advise a person in a position of authority and presents perspectives, ideas, and points of view, for example, when they say, "Father, you have to make the church more appealing, or the parish will not grow."

I respond, without hesitation, "I do not care."

"How could you say that, Father Marc?"

I can say whatever I want because it does not matter. That, beloved in Christ, is *precisely* the lesson. *I* do not matter, *you* do not matter, and *St. Elizabeth's* does not matter—only the lesson matters.

Deep down inside, you want to believe in something you can control, which is what you mean by trust. That is what people love about family—about moms, dads, sons, daughters, brothers, and sisters. When you have a family, you have something stable, safe, and reliable, like a church or a good job.

Unfortunately, the things or people in which you place your trust in exchange for safety and security are false gods—the very gods called to judgment by God in Psalm 82:

> *"God takes his stand in his own congregation; he judges in the midst of the rulers. How long will you judge unjustly and show partiality to the wicked? Vindicate the weak and fatherless; Do justice to the afflicted and destitute. Rescue the weak and needy; Deliver them out of the hand of the wicked. They do not know nor do they understand; They walk about in darkness; All the foundations of the earth are shaken. I*

No Security Blankets

said, "You are gods, and all of you are sons of the Most High. "Nevertheless you will die like men and fall like any one of the princes." Arise, O God, judge the earth! For to you belong all the nations." (Psalm 82)

When we chant this Psalm on Holy Saturday, we wrongly assume it refers to Jesus. On the contrary, the text of the Psalm calls upon Elohim, not the Messiah, to arise in judgment! In the New Testament, the other gods and rulers wrongly condemned Jesus, Elohim's *locum tenens* (himself also a son of man), sentencing him to death.

If we are to hear Psalm 82 correctly in a liturgical context, we must hear it as St. Paul does, namely, that in the Resurrection of Jesus, God is intervening as the only Judge to reverse the ruling of the human court. In Psalm 82, along the lines of Ezekiel and Isaiah, Elohim rises above all the other gods *and his Son* as the *only reference* upon the earth.

Elohim *alone* is the Judge who subdues unjust rulers, those who show partiality to the wicked and dare to condemn *his* Christ. Elohim *alone* is the Judge who vindicates the weak and the fatherless, who cares for the afflicted and the destitute:

"Put not your trust in princes, in sons of men, in whom there is no salvation." (Psalm 146:3)

Your gods are condemned in Psalm 82. They are the earthly princes and sons of men. They will surely die and fall to the ground like any *ben 'adam* (son of man). Their power is a hoax. They are putting on a show for you. They know you trust them because you trust security,

Dark Sayings

safety, comfort, and wealth. They manipulate you to increase your dependence on them. Your trust is grounded in fear!

Take, for instance, the media theatrics surrounding the debt ceiling. Most people possess an innate understanding of an unspoken social contract. You trust your gods, and they deliver stability. It is a game show staged publicly to appease and impress constituencies.

They understand that they must make a deal, or the country will become chaotic. So, they make the deal—and you trust them to make it because they provide security. Read Richard's book on the Prophet Hosea.[36] They provide security by waging war, ensuring you have money in the bank and food in the supermarket. In return, you worship them, and you count on them. That is the agreement. They are your gods. They are the gods in whom you place your trust. Best of all, you can control them, and they allow it. But you have no control over God the Father or those who repeat his words, like Jesus.

God in Scripture is the cause of chaos. He is the one who disrupts your market, destroys your cities, and speaks the words that offend and betray your fake "reference." The Scriptural God is the one who walks out on your Parish Council meeting and says something that someone who "belongs to you" would never say. The Scriptural God does not have any close friends or relatives:

---

[36] Benton, Richard. *The Chrysostom Bible - Hosea: A Commentary.* OCABS Press, 2021.

No Security Blankets

"And it was reported to him, 'Your mother and your brothers are standing outside, wishing to see you.' But he answered and said to them, 'My mother and my brothers are these who hear the word of God and do it.'" (Luke 8:20-21)

Western scholars get caught up with the Twelve Tribes in the Old Testament because their colonial reference is Thomas Jefferson. Unfortunately for them, there is only one Shepherd in the Bible, which means one flock, no matter how many tribes you find.[37] I repeat—one reference—and he was not chosen in an election. If you obey that reference, Jesus may recognize you one day as his mother or brother.

My friends, it is not rocket science.

For those who accept Scripture as their reference, every piece of advice someone brings forward is backward. This is why you hear me say, over and over, that *people cannot hear me*. It is not because I am the smartest person in the room. It is because the reference to which I submit is extremely difficult, and people are

---

[37] The same Hebrew word, *shebet*, refers both to the staff of a shepherd *and* the tribe. The staff of God is the premise, the reference, and the totality, not "the community." In the land of Scripture, which is not your land, does not speak your language, does not conform to your norms, does not eat your food, and does not care about your western values, there is no such thing as a flock in abstraction, let alone a community. There is a shepherd-of-flock, in Hebrew, *ro'eh ṣon*, who carries *his* staff. In Scripture, his *shebet* represents *his* singular authority over the Twelve Tribes, which are but one flock in the wilderness. In Scripture, there is no "we" in family, let alone, "we" the family. There is only, "a voice calling (*qol qore*) in the wilderness." (Isaiah 40:3) "*My sheep* hear *my voice*, and I know them, and they follow me." (John 10:27)

Dark Sayings

stubborn. But as Paul says in Galatians: I will not yield in subjection to you, not even for a moment so that the truth of the gospel will remain with you. (Galatians 2:5) It is not a question of agreeing with what I am saying; It is not formulaic or ideological. It is a question of reference:

> *"For my thoughts are not your thoughts, neither are your ways my ways, declares the Lord." (Isaiah 55:8)*

In the end, your common sense is not God's common sense. If you accept God's common sense, you become an idiot and a fool in the eyes of men. You become illogical. Try it. Try accepting the Scriptural God as your reference and being a corporate executive. Try it. Try accepting the Scriptural God as your reference so that every time you challenge your family, your parish, and your colleagues, the words that come out of your mouth to them sound upside down, and everyone you encounter from your perspective is backward.[38] When people say they trust something, they mean, "I will choose something I consider reliable and safe."

What God promises in Scripture is the only truly reliable thing, but not on your terms. He does not guarantee that the stock market will go up. He does not guarantee that you will be safe and secure. He only offers wisdom—and wisdom that will not necessarily benefit you.

---

[38] "Letting people be wrong about you or a situation while keeping your peace and focus is the most misunderstood power move you will ever make."; https://twitter.com/TheModern Morgan/status/1526936185901285376?lang=en

No Security Blankets

As a pastor, I know from experience that no matter what you say in your human heart, the truth of Scripture is not what you want. If you tell me this is what you want, I will say openly that you are lying to yourself and me. It is not what you want. But it is what you need and what I need. It is also what this society needs, and, as such, it is our burden. Beyond this, it is our duty for the sake of the generation yet unborn.

This is the challenge of Scripture.

That is why, as I said last week, I do not need family, let alone parishioners. What priest, in his right mind, speaks this way? Only a fool. But according to Scripture, the fool says in his heart, "There is no Judge." In other words, the fool is the one who declares, "I am my own reference."[39]

---

[39] To understand the power of the Semitic triliteral root, consider the grammatical, functional, empirical, and, thus, anti-Platonic literary interconnection between **D**a**B**a**R** (word), ke**D**o**BR**am (pasture), ya**DB**e**R** (subdued), watte**D**a**BB**e**R** (destroyed), be**D**a**BB**e**R**o (at his speaking), mi**DB**a**R**ek (your mouth), and mi**DB**a**R** (wilderness). Only in the original Semitic do we hear and see the consonantal link between the shepherd's pasture, the utterances of God, the wilderness, and the subduing—even the destruction—of those who hear his words. "His *dabar* is administered in the wilderness and proceeds from his shepherd's mouth while the sheep's dilemma lies in that the utterly non-Platonic, non-Shakespearian 'to obey or not to obey' is not even the question. It does not matter whether a 'baa' is emitted or not. Obeying maintains the life that the sheep is already enjoying, while disobedience posits the same sheep as *'obed* (unto destruction) as an Aramean by himself in the wilderness."; Tarazi, Paul Nadim. *The Rise of Scripture*. OCABS Press, 2017, p. 296.

Dark Sayings

Beloved in Christ, the Lord is coming. So please, go back and rehear Matthew. Submit to it as your reference—submit to the voice of the Shepherd crying out to you from the wilderness.

T0 GOD ALONE, be the glory, the dominion, and the majesty, always now and ever, and unto ages of ages. Amen.

Christ is in our midst!

I Believe in One God

The recent coronation of the English king was uncanny in its egregious assault on the biblical proclamation of the Resurrection. On the one hand, those who have stayed with this teaching over the years have (hopefully) come to understand that Scripture is a system of cancellation encoded in literary form. It is a divine story given to undermine everything wrought by the hand of humans, shutting down all that we say and do.

We want scriptural wisdom to be pro-human, but it's satirical. It makes fun of us. It criticizes us. We want to make the case that it does so for our sake. But it won't let us. Instead, it insists upon its rule for the sake of the entire creation, of which we humans are but a small part.

In the teaching of the Resurrection, following the line of Isaiah, only God's instruction is allowed to stand out upon the earth. No human being—least of all a king may stand out—hence the crucifixion of Jesus.

With this in mind, if you are trying to avoid transgressing St. Paul's teaching of the anti-Christ, let me give you some helpful advice: Don't make yourself stand out above all others on international screens with costly pomp and flare. Whatever you do, don't invite your subjects to swear fealty to you. Don't publish articles defending meaningless pageantry. Likewise, don't write a book complaining that you don't stand out. Don't do it. And for God's sake, if you must be coronated, please do it quietly and not during the Paschal season, when we are warned repeatedly that there is only One whom the Father has anointed to stand out upon the earth:

"And he shall come again with glory to judge the living and the dead, and his kingdom shall have no end." (Nicene Creed)

Call No Human Being Your Father

(Homily, Sunday, June 18, 2023)

In the name of the Father, and of the Son, and of the Holy Spirit. Amen.

Christ is in our midst!

The text of Scripture is unbearably intelligent. No one today—least of all, our cancel culture—could withstand the "dark sayings" (Psalm 78) of Scripture's divine comedy, which tears down everything by paying singular homage to the Father of Jesus Christ.

The New Testament gospels of Jesus may resemble the Hero's Journey of Greek literature, but it's a hoax—a bait and switch played on the Roman Empire. As consumers of Hellenism, the Greco-Romans expected a hero like Jason or Heracles. Instead, they got an ordinary functionary, Jesus Christ.

Like all teachers, the biblical writers had no control over their audience, but that did not stop them from coopting and emasculating the Greek monomyth from the inside out.

Doing what the Nicene Creed refused to do, subsequent generations of Greco-Roman theologians fell into the trap of Hellenism, turning Jesus into a hero by putting the Son on the same level as his Father.

Dark Sayings

Christians love to complain about the disrespect of elders in Western culture, but the truth is, it is all our fault. We buy into the logic of Disney because we—the builders of Hagia Sophia—created it. Still, we should know better.

In our tradition, when two or more priests are present, or when a bishop is present among his priests, you may not ask for a blessing from each priest, let alone your preferred cleric. You may only seek the blessing of the elder. The functionary is not the subject.

As I said last week, by ignoring what is written in Psalm 82, we Orthodox have lost the meaning of our own liturgy. The actual service of Holy Saturday is much more powerful than the version we end up with after tamping Scripture down with humanism and Western individualism.

There is a parallel between the parable of the Prodigal Son in Luke and the reading of Psalm 82 on Holy Saturday. As you have heard me say many times, the story's point is the Father's unprecedented act of mercy, not the Prodigal Son's "journey."

The Prodigal was a pretentious, disobedient, underserving jerk, undone by his own sins. His entitled stay-at-home brother was no better. Nevertheless, the Father, the Judge, stood up from his throne and made the shocking decision to greet his wayward son and welcome him home. Jesus, on the other hand, was undone by obedience.

In Luke, by the time Jesus reaches the Mount of Olives, he knows everything is a total loss. He goes so far as to beg for a release from duty because he knows that

I Believe in One God

the will of his Father portends personal ruin.[40] Jesus did everything he was told, yet his prospects were far worse than the most despicable character from one of his own parables. From the perspective of the New Testament, in Psalm 82, it is Jesus, not David, who cries out in desperation, "Arise, O Elohim, judge the earth!" In his commentary on Philippians, Father Paul explains:

"Crucifixion was a death unto total oblivion of someone whose life was unworthy of remembrance: an unworthy end of an unworthy life, shame ending in shame. This is precisely what Paul found in Isaiah 52:13-53:12: an incredible story. God's chosen one, his "slave," is raised from an unimpressive death, that of a slaughtered lamb, into a position of power that surpasses that of mighty kings."[41]

"Who has believed what we have heard? And to whom has the arm of the Lord been revealed?" (Isaiah 53:1)

Jesus was wrongly judged by the sons of the Most High, the gods and rulers on the earth. Mere functionaries—arrogant human beings—the builders of Babel—who "grasp" like stooges at equality with God. In stark contrast, Jesus:

"Though he was in the form of God, did not count equality with God a thing to be grasped, but emptied himself, taking the form of a slave, being born in the likeness of men. And

---

[40] Like the unpleasant incident in Luke 2:48, this fact (Luke 22:41-44) is conveniently ignored or glossed over by Sunday School "curricula," which inevitably replace the Jesus of Scripture with their Greco-Roman statue.

[41] Tarazi, Paul Nadim. *The Chrysostom Bible - Philippians: A Commentary*. OCABS Press, 2009, p. 123.

Dark Sayings

being found in human form, he humbled himself and became obedient unto death, even death on a cross. Therefore God has highly exalted him and bestowed on him the name which is above every name, that at the name of Jesus, every knee should bow, in heaven and on earth and under the earth, and every tongue confess that Jesus Christ is Lord, to the glory of God the Father." (Philippians 2:4–11)

"To the glory of God the Father."

I would like to tell you a story about a recent interaction with my daughter's principal. I was present at her graduation from an alternative school she was fortunate to attend. I was so impressed with the teachers' work that I congratulated the principal following the ceremony. I always congratulate the teacher, never, under any circumstances, the graduate. I introduced myself and said, "Thank you, principal, for all your hard work and everything you and your staff have done for these students." A simple "you're welcome" would have been great. Instead, the unbearable question came after the obligatory flash of fake midwestern humility:

"Who do you belong to?"

Most of you do not recognize the question's absurdity because, like the arrogant gods in Psalm 82 and every human being who has ever lived, you want the Son and the Father to be equal because, like the Emperors of Rome, you want to be God. That is why, deep down inside, Americans enjoy watching Disney sitcoms where kids make fun of their parents. You are like the Greco-Roman theologians, who emphasize Christ in a way that empties the Cross of its power because you covet power—and you do not even realize it.

I Believe in One God

After a brief pause, I answered her.

"Leylah[42] is my daughter."

I do not "belong" to my daughter. My daughter pertains to me. I am *her* reference.

People tell Leylah, "Your mother looks like you." Once again, people have it backward. The daughter looks like the mother. The child pertains to the womb from which it originates. Period.

I explained to Sebastian this morning that in Arabic, a male in his prime is never referred to except in reference to the one who produced him or the one he produced. In Arabic, until you can rear children, you are no reference.

Following this tradition, in reference to his dad, Sebastian is introduced as the "Son of Nicholas" or, in Bedouin fashion, before he has children, as the "Father of Nicholas." A form of pressure, the latter is said in anticipation that Sebastian will take responsibility for a family in the future, continuing his father's household. In an American setting, you might ask, "Why so much pressure?"

As St. Paul says, "because the days are evil," and time is precious. As such, you are no longer Sebastian. Starting today, I call you "Papa" because the time is coming when you must provide for others. But

---

[42] *Leylah*, in Arabic and Hebrew, means "night," a name given to one born at night. In the Arab world, a central theme of folkloric music and fellowship; in Arabic and Persian literature, a woman of spellbinding beauty. It's literary counterpart, *majnūn* (crazy, overcome by passion) is taken from the name of her suitor.

Dark Sayings

remember, you have a father, so ultimately, you are no reference. Your father is the one who pressures you, and he will always be above you.

"A disciple is not above his teacher, nor a slave above his master." (Matthew 10:24)

That is what is meant by this system of saying the "father of" or the "son of." When I call Sebastian by his father's name, I tell him, "Son, you have work to do. You are no big deal. You are not the reference."

Sebastian is a functionary. A *ben 'adam*. He is either being produced or producing. Beyond that, he is of no value to God.

But we Americans believe that Leylah as an individual is useful because she exists. There it is—that ugly Platonic word, "existence."[43] I just want "to be."

Now, if you have ever managed a store or had a real job like St. Paul, where you are responsible for producing or doing anything before God, nothing is more irritating than a person on the clock charging you an hourly fee who just wants "to be."

Jesus was not useful because he "existed." As the Son of his Father, he was useful because, as St. Paul proclaims, under extreme pressure, he "emptied himself, taking the form of a slave…and became

---

[43] "Existence" as in the verb "to be," is not found in Semetic languages. The Greek *existēmi* and the Latin *existo* literally mean "stand out."; Tarazi, Paul Nadim. *The Rise of Scripture*. OCABS Press, 2017, p. 77.

obedient unto death." He did what his Father asked, even when he realized it meant personal ruin.

That is why his Father got up from his throne on Holy Saturday—to judge all the other power-grasping gods who condemned the Messiah, undoing their lies once and for all.

So, call no human being your father on Father's Day because Elohim is the only Father, King, Power, and Reference.

Technically, when you see the icon of the Pantokrator on the ceiling, it is a misrepresentation because, in the gospels, Jesus does not come seated in power like George Washington.[44] On the contrary, in the text, he is always "seated at the right hand of Power"[45] because, without exception, all power belongs to the Father. You do not like it, and I do not like it. Constantine and Justinian hated it. But that is how the Bible works:

"Not to us, O Lord, not to us, but to your name give glory. Because of your lovingkindness, because of your truth. Why should the nations say, "Where, now, is their God?" But our God is in the heavens; He does whatever he pleases." (Psalm 115:1–3)

To him alone, be the glory, the dominion, and the majesty, always now and ever, and unto ages of ages. Amen.

Christ is in our midst!

---

[44] Wikipedia contributors. "The Apotheosis of Washington." *Wikipedia*, May 2023, en.wikipedia.org/wiki/%20The_Apotheosis _of_Washington.
[45] Matthew 26:64; Mark 14:62.

Disobey Your Thirst

Suppose you ask an American what's wrong with the culture and have enough patience to wade through people's anger and cheap sound bites. You'll find surprising agreement across all ideological boundaries: something is broken. Even those hell-bent on defending American exceptionalism will eventually contradict themselves and blame someone for why things are not as great as they should be. People feel a sense of loss.

Whatever they believe, no matter how they answer, underneath it all is a deep sadness (often masked by anger) that few can put their finger on. Life is not our property. It does not belong to us. Yet we persist in behaving otherwise. The belief that we are its proprietors controls our treatment of each other and the natural world. It thrusts the insanity upon us that everything exists for us. This belief is empirically insane, yet we accept it and then act confused as the damage around us accelerates.

This sin of modern man, who demands obedience from life, was codified in 1994 in the marketing slogan, "obey your thirst."[46] It's unclear whether the saying influenced the culture or expressed what we had already become. In my experience as a priest, when modern Christians talk about obedience, they unwittingly reference this Coca-Cola slogan, not Scripture. "Humbly," they obey their thirst, channeling water away from the oasis to the city, fulfilling their selfish

---

[46] Muse, Tyler. "The Untold Story of Sprite's 'Obey Your Thirst' Slogan." *History Oasis*, www.historyoasis.com/ post/obey-your-thirst. Accessed 28 July 2023.

Disobey Your Thirst

purpose. In God's eyes, on this point, the English language is broken. It is the human being, not the so-called wilderness, that is "wild." It is the will of the human being that must submit to life, not the other way around.

Glorify Your Father and Mother

(Homily, Sunday, June 25, 2023)

In the name of the Father, and of the Son, and of the Holy Spirit. Amen.

Christ is in our midst!

In Romans 5, St. Paul speaks openly of boasting about suffering, not for the first time. In Romans, 1 Corinthians 4, and elsewhere, he does so, in part, to illustrate that he does not share the same reference as his addressees.

In Roman Corinth, his followers, not unlike American believers, are so filled with their own spirit (more like "full of it" if you catch Paul's wordplay) that they are unable to see the needs of the weaker brother, staring them right in the face. So, when they boast about their god, fake spirit, or wisdom or claim that they understand what Paul is saying, they are not talking about Paul's teaching; they are talking about themselves.

They do not share the same reference as Paul.

That is why when they boast about grace or being filled with the spirit, they boast like idiots who have never received anything from Paul; because, in their arrogance, they demonstrate to the "Small Apostle" that they have not been put to shame yet. Hence, Paul's mighty letter reads like a pastoral instruction manual on weaponizing shame against the church.

Still—even in 1 Corinthians—Paul does not boast of his suffering strictly to shame the arrogant. On the contrary, when he vaunts his tribulations, he does so to clarify his point of reference as the basis for his preaching. His suffering pertains not to his personal experience but to the content of the teaching of the Cross, which brings great shame upon the church. What follows in 1 Corinthians is typical of any Roman household under the authority of its Patrician: the father increases in glory, and his children decrease—in Paul's letter, not for the glory of Caesar, but to the glory of God the Father, through Jesus Christ. This is the sole function of biblical preaching, lost to modern pastors and churches, who coddle one another with platitudes about love to increase their income. St. Paul exclaims:

"We are fools for Christ's sake, but you are wise in Christ; we are weak, but you are strong; you are distinguished, but we are without honor. To this present hour, we are both hungry and thirsty, and are poorly clothed, and are roughly treated, and are homeless; and we toil, working with our own hands; when we are reviled, we bless; when we are persecuted, we endure; when we are slandered, we try to conciliate; we have become as the scum of the world, the dregs of all things, even until now." (1 Corinthians 4:10-13)

For the Small Apostle, the church's arrogance can only be undone if its members obey the teaching to which his suffering bears witness. It is this teaching of which he boasts. They will only then understand that they, not Paul, have everything backward. So, Paul begins his letter with this end in mind, correcting their false reference for boasting as if to say:

> *I, Paul, the teacher, not you, am wise in the gospel. To the self-referential (arrogant and impressive Americans like you), I may look foolish and weak, but you have it backward because you are the ones who have rejected the teaching of the Cross as your reference. I am strong and powerful in the teaching of Jesus Christ, which looks crazy to you because you have no clue about the content of this teaching. What I lack in worldly gain and comfort, I have all the more in the hope of the coming Kingdom—and that is precisely what I am bragging about: The Kingdom of the Most High God. I do not pertain to your foolish worldly reference. My hope and bragging are in the Father of Jesus Christ and his coming Kingdom. I rejoice when I am ridiculed. I bless your enemies and the enemies of your friends, which makes me hated by everyone, including you. You cannot possibly love me. I am an embarrassment to you. I love you and honor you with this teaching, heaping coals on your head. This is a cause for greater boasting in God's eyes because my bragging refers—not to me—but to the teaching of Scripture.*

In Romans 5, Paul makes a similar point. In this case, it does not concern human arrogance and the teaching of the Cross but the hope of God's peace (the coming Judgment) as his singular reference. According to Paul, the God who rescued us on the day of Grace (when we were beyond rescue) has the power to save us on the day of Peace. The fact that Paul now endures tribulation confirms this teaching, which promises that our trust in this same God will be tested on the path to Judgment:

Dark Sayings

"We also boast in our tribulations, knowing that tribulation brings about perseverance; and perseverance, proven character; and proven character, hope; and hope does not disappoint because the love of God has been poured out within our hearts through the Holy Spirit who was given to us. For while we were still helpless, at the right time, Christ died for the ungodly. For one will hardly die for a righteous man, though perhaps for the good man, someone would dare even to die. But God demonstrates his own love toward us, in that while we were yet sinners, Christ died for us. Much more then, having now been justified by his blood, we shall be saved from the wrath of God through him." (Romans 5:3-9)

In both examples, Paul's boasting is not self-referential. Still, I know from experience that whenever Paul refers to his own suffering, all we Americans can hear is the ongoing competition inside our heads over who holds the title of the "ultimate victim."

I know because, after years of preaching this teaching, people have responded, to my face, without fail, "Oh yeah, well, I suffer too," or, "I suffer more." Never once does the question of reference enter anyone's mind. Everyone's interest is power.

Their power.

Their suffering points not to Scripture but to themselves (their family, business, job, life story, ideology, or whatever) as their reference, which weakens Paul and strengthens them, emptying the Cross of *its* power.

All of us are about power. Some people are honest about this. The rest lie to themselves or hide behind politically correct platitudes, which Ezekiel and

Disobey Your Thirst

Matthew refer to as "whitewash." [47] Ultimately, everyone operates under the lust for power as a survival mechanism.

Each time you walk through St. Elizabeth's doors, you are confronted with the tyranny of your power, which rules your life in open rebellion against the freedom of the Kingdom of the heavens.

Even as Paul boasts about his suffering, you play the victim, imagining that Paul, the Apostle of Jesus Christ, feels sorry for himself.

You fool!

Paul is preaching the hope of the Kingdom, that through his obedience to Jesus Christ, all power will be taken away from every human being who has ever lived and transferred to God the Father in the final Judgment.

His hope does not rest on the significance of his suffering, the fact that he experienced it, or the belief that human suffering or his story carries profound meaning. It is not about learning from his suffering. Nor is it about gaining legitimacy through suffering or the ability to blame others, which is why you Americans vent to your therapist.

On the contrary, his hope and rejoicing lie in that his suffering pertains not to himself or his story but to the content of the book standing upright on the altar table behind me!

That is what is meant by the term "witness!"

---

[47] Ezekiel 13:10-15; Matthew 23:27

Dark Sayings

Unlike the gossip about yourself, which is vain talk, the tribulation of which he boasts is for the sake of the gospel!

We Christians will never accept or comprehend that the only thing in human civilization not about our power is the divine teaching that strips us of power.

It does so by canceling self-reference, which we will never accept. Everything in the world is acceptable to humans, except for Paul's teaching, which is the endurance of hope under the pressure of our utter and complete cancellation:

"Far be it from me to boast except in the Cross of our Lord Jesus Christ, by which the world has been crucified to me, and I to the world." (Galatians 6:14)

As a young priest, I endeavored to explain this concept to an individual attempting to persuade me that my sermons conveyed an authoritarian arrogance that would ultimately damage my reputation.

Definitely and defiantly, I replied: To strip human beings of power, Scripture takes all power and authority to itself. The Scriptural God—literally—clothes himself with arrogance and pride (*geut*)[48] so that we human beings cannot do the same—and we hate him for it.

As the Orthodox say (with respect to Confession), you cannot have a personal relationship with your invisible

---

[48] Yahweh is clothed with arrogance (*geut*). (Psalm 93:1); The wicked (*rasha*) does not *ra'a* (Hebrew, "perceive," Arabic, "see, deem true") the arrogance (*geut*) of Yahweh. (Isaiah 26:10)

Disobey Your Thirst

friend. Power must have a reference. You cannot glorify your imaginary friend. As the Good Book says:

> *"Glorify your father and your mother, that your days may be prolonged in the land which the Lord your God gives you." (Exodus 20:12)*

It does not say, "honor your father and mother," as typically translated. The verb *kabad*, from the root *kabod*, refers to glory or weightiness. We are commanded to glorify the authority set above us.[49] This rule from the same God who demands that we place our confidence solely in his teaching and not in our parents, whom he calls:

> *"A stubborn and rebellious generation, a generation that did not prepare its heart and whose spirit was not faithful to God." (Psalm 78:8)*

"Tribulation brings about perseverance."

It does not matter if your parents, priest, teacher, boss, or anyone set above you are wicked or righteous. According to Scripture, they are set above you by God. So, give away your glory to them in anticipation of the Kingdom, and endure under pressure, "knowing that tribulation brings about perseverance; and perseverance, proven character; and proven character, hope; and hope does not disappoint because the love of God has been poured out within our hearts through the

---

[49] Ishak, my father's middle name, passed down by his fathers, means "he laughs" in Hebrew, as in, God is laughing at us. I miss you dad.; Cosmopolitan. *Why so Many Young People Are Cutting off Their Parents.* apple.news/Aj-gAYbdnRwa1HTelwIG25g.

Dark Sayings

Holy Spirit who was given to us. For while we were still helpless, at the right time, Christ died for the ungodly."

And please, remember that when Paul speaks of the ungodly, he refers to you and me, not the authorities we dislike.

You are stuck with the tangible reference God gives you, through whom you transfer all glory to our only reference, God the Father of our Lord Jesus Christ. This is how the subjugation of Christ himself functions for us:

"When all things are subjected to him, then the Son himself also will be subjected to the One who subjected all things to him, so that God [the Father] *may be all in all."* (1 Corinthians 15:28)

The Bible is a chain of command. Period. This "personal relationship with God" nonsense is anti-scriptural. Your relationship is with your parents. That is why the classic Roman prayer concludes with the scriptural formula: "*Through Jesus Christ,* our Lord. Amen." Even then, technically, only Paul may pray "through Christ." The rest of us are further down the pecking order. The Father may be our only reference, but we are consigned to deal with his local patrician, whoever that may be. That is how your parents, priest, boss, or elder of any kind function for you under the power of Scripture.

Whoever you are stuck with, your reference is not the individual themself, but the content of the book standing upright on the altar table behind me!

Reference!

Disobey Your Thirst

As I have explained many times, *kabod*, in Hebrew, refers to the weight of the statue in the temple. The greater the god, the bigger and heavier its statue, the greater its glory. Along these lines, *kabod* can also refer to the weight of spoils captured in war. These, too, increase the king's glory: more treasure, bigger temple, heavier statue.

In human terms, when you preach about the glory of your god, your reference is the size of John Ireland's cathedral or St. Elizabeth's church. You are still "full of it," like the members of Paul's church in Roman Corinth.

When Scripture proclaims the glory of God, it refers to a deity that you cannot see, let alone weigh on human scales of glory, who presents his Son as an irrelevant man who led an unremarkable life, shamed and spit upon by all, only to be vindicated and raised by his unseen Father, in a Resurrection, once again, that you did not see and cannot measure, let alone depict.

Your "treasure" is in the heavens.

Are you getting it yet?

We are commanded to transfer all glory to this unseen God, who has no visible reference except his written teaching, which appoints as its *locum tenens* the parents and worldly authorities that you *can* see and the tribulations that you *do* experience in this life. All these become God's leverage against you, to strip you of your power in the hope of his promise.

Dark Sayings

Then, in a clever twist of irony (or so it seems), Jesus says, "Do not call anyone on earth your father; for you have one Father, who is in heaven." (Matthew 23:9)

Now, because you love power, when confronted with the weight of God's authority imposed upon you by Scripture through your father, the priest, you mumble to yourself, "I thought Jesus opposed power. He said, 'Call no man your father.'"

Yes, beloved in Christ, and I thought Judas loved the poor.

Unfortunately for you and me, the only people in our life (knowingly or unknowingly) able to play the part of Pontius Pilate for our sake are those who have power over us. Only through them can we submit to the will of the Father. They are the Scriptural God's real-world patricians assigned to keep us under constant pressure in tribulation, putting God's words back in our faces until the time of the promise. That is why Paul, himself the slave of Jesus Christ, assumes the role of a Roman Patrician in 1 Corinthians:

"For though you have countless guides in Christ, you do not have many fathers. For I became your father in Christ Jesus through the gospel." (1 Corinthians 4:15)

That is how authority works in Scripture. Suddenly, you find yourself in a situation where you are commanded to glorify God through the person set above you who is equally powerless in his own right.

To the only wise God, through Jesus Christ, be the glory forever. Amen.

Christ is in our midst!

The *Toledot* of Elohim

From the beginning, the Scriptural God commanded biological reproduction—be fruitful and multiply. Reproduce biologically because the generation yet unborn cannot be created by studying or preaching the Torah. But remember that God is King, and they are his children, not yours. But the human beings did not listen. Cain multiplied himself, raising offspring to his own dynasty, dedicating Encoch and his seed—not to God's commandments—but to buildings of stone. This situation did not last very long.

After the flood, God established the oneness of the human race through Noah's sons, demonstrating his intention that the nations live alongside each other under his rule. Among them was Shem, the forbear of Abraham, "by whom" God said, "all the families of the earth" shall be blessed. All. From the sons of Noah to the settlement in Canaan, the Israelites were destined to live alongside the Gentiles already dwelling in Canaan, yes, Canaan, the term artificially doubled by Luke at the climax of his genealogy.

The stage was set from the beginning. Israel was never special or exceptional. They were one nation among many honored by Elohim with the special gift of his teaching. In the same way, the "prophet Jesus from Nazareth of Galilee" (Matthew 21:11) had a special duty when God sent him to complete the work begun by Jonah of sharing this teaching.

From Genesis to Revelation—the Bible is not Adam's story, Noah's, Abraham's, or Shem's, let alone Israel's; even David needed reminding when the Lord struck

The Toledot of Elohim

down his child by Bathsheba: Elohim is King and Judge. It is his dynasty, and they are his children, not yours.

In obedience to Elohim, Jesus, the unremarkable human being, refused the throne. Jesus, the Lord with no army, property, children, or *toledot*. Jesus, the last of the prophets, who rejected everything Herod represents and went on to die a loser, in total shame, with no value in human terms.

Whom We Do Not See

(Homily, Sunday, July 2, 2023)

In the name of the Father, and of the Son, and of the Holy Spirit. Amen.

Christ is in our midst!

I have been emphasizing something difficult for people to accept: the absolute centrality of having a physical, tangible, in-the-flesh reference for a God who is invisible and unseen.

There is a biblical saying from 1 John that I like, one often quoted by St. Elizabeth, and I have emphasized it from the day that Archbishop Job assigned her as our patron:

> *"If anyone says, 'I love God,' and hates his brother, he is a liar; for he who does not love his brother whom he has seen cannot love God, whom he has not seen." (1 John 4:20)*

In English translations of the New Testament, whenever you hear the word "God," you must not think of Jesus, the Son of God. Instead, always connect the word "God" with the Hebrew term "Elohim," which

Dark Sayings

pertains specifically to the Father, our only reference. On this point, Arabic speakers have an advantage [50] because, as a contraction of the generic "*el-ilah*," the specific "Allah" corresponds to Elohim, the Father, above all the gods in Psalm 82.

Once again, the important thing about Elohim is that he cannot be weighed or measured. You cannot see or touch him. So, when 1 John talks about the God whom you do not see, it refers to the Father of Jesus, Elohim. In the Torah (Instruction or Law), Nevi'im (Prophets), and the Ketuvim (Writings) of the Old Testament, the generic English term "god" is nowhere to be found.

Beloved in Christ, my intention is not to ridicule the English language, which is beautiful and proud in its own right. I am not ridiculing English per se, but mocking it, in a specific way, with respect to Scripture.

God does not speak English.[51]

---

[50] "With respect to Hebrew lexicography, the "great reservoir" of Arabic literature and vocabulary has not been dealt with satisfactorily."; Guillaume, Alfred. *Hebrew and Arabic Lexicography: A Comparative Study.* Brill Archive, 1965, p. 1.; Centuries earlier, Ibn Barun, a Jewish Rabbi and famed grammarian of al-Andalus, produced his great work, *The Book of Comparison Between the Hebrew and the Arabic Languages.* It was his conviction that because Arabic continued as a living Semitic language, it was invaluable for providing insight into the biblical text and for the comparative study of Hebrew.; Wechter, Pinchas. *Ibn Barun's Arabic Works on Hebrew Grammar and Lexicography.* 1964.

[51] St. Jerome explains that the translator of the Bible, "like a conqueror…has led away captive into his own tongue the meaning of his originals." (Letter 57) The spoken language of a people

The Toledot *of Elohim*

English is not a sacred language. If you accept Scripture as your reference, English can never be a holy language. My statement is not an opinion. It is a literary and historical fact, a technical statement. God speaks

---

reflects a practical reality, meaning the way that things work in daily life out of what God himself forms in the womb. Spoken language is not manufactured; it is found. In Semitic languages, this is especially powerful because of the phenomenon of the triliteral root. The special value of a sacred written text, specifically the consonantal Hebrew of the Bible and the Arabic Qur'an, is that the practical reality of its language at the time of its writing is fixed. To the extent that the biblical text itself concocts *its* scriptural Hebrew as "a cross of the different (extant) Semitic languages" (Paul Nadim Tarazi, The Rise of Scripture, p. 68) it is not so much the Hebrew language as it is the *Semitic language of God* encoded in the Bible. In other words, the Bible, *including the New Testament*, is written in God's Semitic *debarim*. Combined with the living tradition of spoken Arabic, whose triliteral functionality is preserved in the fixed text of the Qur'an, this fact makes the everyday spoken Arabic of simple people of more value in the study of consonantal biblical Hebrew than the most expensive theological degrees from the fanciest schools. One need only hear a secular teacher of Arabic from the land—as Jerome said, "led away captive," explain lexicology and grammar as she teaches Arabic. Even if she is not interested in the Bible or the Qur'an, she cannot help but share knowledge of more value for the hearing of the same than what modern religious scholarship can offer because of what is found in the etymology of the language, which is itself sacred. "Translation," Robert Carrol explains, is a "transformation" that "wrenches the text from its home in the ancient cultures and languages, deports that text, and exiles it in foreign languages and cultures."; Carroll, Robert P. "Cultural Encroachment and Bible Translation: Observations on Elements of Violence, Race and Class in the Production of Bibles in Translation." *Semeia*, edited by Randall C. Bailey and Tina Pippin, vol. 76, Society of Biblical Literature, 1996, p. 40.

Dark Sayings

Hebrew, and to our visitors today, our beloved sisters from Yemen, he speaks Arabic.[52]

Never a word in English.

And when he speaks—in Scripture—it is clear that his name, Elohim, is interchangeable with the term "Judge."

God is the Judge. That is why, regarding Elohim, there is always an emphasis on parenting. But how can an invisible person in the heavens put pressure on you or scold you? How can such a one parent you?

It is impossible.

If you live in this country, more than likely, you have accepted the modern lie that your imaginary friend can

---

[52] Peter T. Daniels proposed the Arabic term "abjad" to describe a type of Semitic script "that denotes individual consonants only," forcing the reader to infer vowel sounds as they read the text. The term abjad is derived from the original (pre-Islamic) order of the first four letters of the Arabic alphabet (ʾalif, bāʾ, jīm, dāl), which correspond to other Semitic languages, notably, "Hebrew and Semitic proto-alphabets: specifically, aleph, bet, gimel, and dalet." Insofar as the Masoretic was vocalized by someone else, its fidelity to the original is as much an interpretation as any English translation. The answer is not a better translation. The solution is for modern disciples of the Bible to submit to the original, unvocalized Hebrew text, reading Hebrew without vowels in the same way that modern Arabs read the morning newspaper, which is printed without vowels. Only then will students of the Bible be liberated from the tyranny of the tower builders of Genesis 11, who impose control through their interpretations, part and parcel of their imperial languages.; Wikipedia contributors. "Abjad." *Wikipedia*, July 2023, en.wikipedia.org/wiki/Abjad#cite_note-4.; Daniels, Peter T. "Fundamentals of Grammatology." *Journal of the American Oriental Society*, vol. 110, no. 4, 1990, pp. 727-731.

The **Toledot** *of Elohim*

indeed parent you as long as you follow the correct "idea" in a book. Then, as the deacon explained this morning, like all idealists, you live as you please, even as you "read" the Bible. You are free. No one can tell you anything. You imagine that you are under God. But you do not trust in Elohim, the Scriptural God. As an American, you trust in the power of your dollar.

Your currency is your reference.

Ten years [53] after you dropped the bomb on the Japanese—within days of the anniversary of that holocaust—your congress inscribed the words "in God we trust" on your currency.[54]

You took those three letters, g-o-d, which have nothing to do with the Bible and made the dollar bill your parent. Since then, each time you put your hand in your pocket, you take your talisman out and gaze lovingly at your pocket-god, in whom you trust.

Congress gave you a reference.

But your false god is not a judge. He is not an enforcer. He is an enabler who helps and encourages you to chase after your lusts and pursue your happiness. The sin of Jeffersonian freedom is slavery to yourself. As Deacon Anthony said correctly this morning, such freedom is condemned by Paul in Galatians; it is slavery to

---

[53] Wikipedia contributors. "Atomic Bombings of Hiroshima and Nagasaki." *Wikipedia*, July 2023, en.wikipedia.org/wiki/Atomic_bombings_of_Hiroshima_and_Nagasaki.

[54] Wikipedia contributors. "In God We Trust." *Wikipedia*, July 2023, en.wikipedia.org/wiki/In_God_We_Trust.

Dark Sayings

Pharaoh. *You* are Pharaoh. Just ask the unseen people of Yemen. But it feels so good.

This is the difficulty of Scripture—the precise point where Greco-Roman and Western theologians, seduced by Neoplatonism, trip over themselves: The physical demands imposed by Scripture, like the physical act of giving birth in the flesh, do not feel good.

So, the Neoplatonists twist Galatians, insisting that you can follow God and become his son or daughter in a vacuum without producing physical offspring. This is utterly laughable, like the fantasy of being "physically" spanked by an unseen and bodiless parent who dwells in the heavens.

Human beings do not appear out of nowhere neatly arranged on a sterile shelf at your local brick-and-mortar store, complete with a warranty and return policy. But that is what people want and how Americans now behave. In Genesis, Elohim thunders:

> *"Be fruitful and multiply and fill the earth and subdue it; and have dominion over the fish of the sea and over the birds of the air and over every living thing that moves upon the earth." (Genesis 1:27)*

The Hebrew terms "subdue," *kabash*, and "have dominion over," *radah* are indelibly linked with the ordinance to serve *'abad* (slave to), and keep, *shamar* (protect) the earth.

Elohim's will in Genesis is that his dominion over creation is to be expressed through a regular *ben 'adam* (an ordinary human being), who is born and multiplies sexually, like any other mammal, thus canceling the

The Toledot *of Elohim*

need for the arrogant rulers and "sons of God," referred to in Psalm 82.

That is why a few verses later, the human being who supposedly "has dominion" is put under pressure by Elohim as a slave. In Genesis, in a twist that is reflected throughout St. Paul's letters, the temporal sons of men "rule" under pressure as slaves in God's household:

"Then the Lord God took the man and put him into the garden of Eden to serve (slave to) it and keep (protect) it." (Genesis 2:15)

Why is this such an important commandment?

To the American mind, mercy is conceptual, even idyllic, as though a person can "feel" mercy and "act" upon it. From the perspective of Genesis, this is nonsensical. In Scripture, mercy is linguistically entangled, not with feeling or thought, but with the pressure of physical childbirth.

Beloved in Christ, those who grew up in the United States after World War II have little or no chance of understanding the Bible. Those who did not, or people from places like Yemen—where entitlement is not an indelible premise—understand that having a coffee with your dad is a job, not a treat or a form of entertainment.

For such people, coffee with your dad is pressure. A few of the elderly at St. Elizabeth's, I am sure, understand me. Spending time with your parents in those days was pressure. It was not fun. Your dad was your judge.

Dark Sayings

This is the pressure through which Scripture propagates itself for your sake.

The Scriptures, which cancel mighty kings and princes in Genesis, are not interested in your family or the silly honor of your father and mother. The Bible hates dynasties. It ridicules your parents and cancels your power.

When you honor your parents, as the commandment is wrongly translated, you lift yourself up. You are to *glorify your parents* so that you are *put to shame* through their weightiness.

The Bible is interested in downward pressure. Scripture's sole objective is the propagation of God's instruction. As such, it uses whatever it can to pressure us to carry out this instruction.

So yes, the Bible is about the spread of God's seed. But you cannot do what the Neoplatonists and theologians do by saying, "Oh well then, it's not really about making babies; it's about making disciples."

No. *Definitely not.* You are not eternal gods. You cannot "make" anything. Moreover, Jesus warns, when you do, "you make them twice as much a child of hell as yourselves." (Matthew 23:15)

You are flesh and blood creatures born of a mother, as God commands in Genesis. You have no choice in the matter. That is the genius of the Bible. You must multiply sexually like any other mammal because you "will die…and fall like any prince." (Psalm 82) Although Cain desperately tried, you cannot get around this through dynasty or by dedicating your children to cities

The **Toledot** *of Elohim*

and monuments. It is the words of Elohim—his seed—not your silly eternity projects, that stand forever:

> *"A voice says, 'Call out.' Then he answered, 'What shall I call out?' All flesh is grass, and all its loveliness is like the flower of the field. The grass withers, the flower fades, when the breath of the Lord blows upon it; The people are indeed grass! The grass withers, the flower fades, but the word of our God stands forever." (Isaiah 40:6-9)*

In the Old Testament, the sons of Cain tried to circumvent human transience by building monuments to themselves (statues, temples, cities, etc.) as though a temple of stone in Manhattan built in the shape of a mother's womb could replace the lives lost on 9/11.

"Shame," cries Isaiah! "Shame!" "Shame," laments Jeremiah! Is this what you learned from the fall of the Twin Towers? Even Rachel cannot weep for you. The Prophet David himself condemns us:

> *"As for man, his days are like grass; Like a flower of the field, so he flourishes. When the wind has passed over it, it is gone, and its place no longer knows about it. But the mercy of the Lord is from everlasting to everlasting for those who fear him, and his justice to the children's children, to those who keep his covenant and remember his commandments, to do them." (Psalm 103:15-17)*

In Scripture, the mercy of the Lord is expressed not in stone monuments and buildings but in the opening of a woman's flesh-and-blood womb. As God commands, a woman becomes a mother when her blood is shed, giving away life so another can receive life. In stark

Dark Sayings

contrast, men take life in the building of monuments and the defense of their cities.

Just ask the children of Yemen, whom we Americans do not see.[55]

In Hebrew, mercy, *raḥamim* is the plural form of womb, *reḥem*. The same words, mercy and womb, are also interlocked in Arabic, *as intended by God*, the merciful (*al-raḥim*) and the compassionate (*al-raḥmān*).

God lives, and life will continue only as he intends, not by the hand of man or the words of man's mouth, but from everlasting to everlasting, through the dominion of his rule over all:

> *"But when the fullness of the time had come, God sent his Son, born of a woman, born under the Law, so that he might redeem those who were under the Law, that we might receive the adoption as sons." (Galatians 4:4-5)*

---

[55] Chris Hedges, criticizing "the deification of American history and the Founding Fathers" in an interview with Briahna Joy Gray explained: "Having spent twenty years outside the [American] Empire in places like El Salvador and the Middle East I can tell you there are a lot of Iraqis and Palestinians and Salvadorans who don't think we as a country are particularly good given the plethora of crimes that we have committed against those 'friends,' who I'll call the 'Wretched of the Earth.' The Empire is a pretty evil entity, and of course, as James Baldwin pointed out, we choose not to look at Empire, and we confuse (I'm quoting Baldwin of course), we confuse ignorance with innocence, and then as Baldwin said, that eventually turns you into a monster."; Bad Faith. "Chris Hedges on Cornel West 2024, RFK Jr., Green Party Strategy." *YouTube*, 22 June 2023, www.youtube.com/watch?v=8i9BKJR9Nro.

The Toledot *of Elohim*

To him alone, be the glory, the dominion, and the majesty, always now and ever, and unto ages of ages. Amen.

Christ is in our midst!

(Note: Ravaged by war since 2014, 80% of the population of Yemen lives below the poverty line. 4.5 million people have lost their communities and homes. More than 11 million children need humanitarian assistance; 2.2 million suffer from acute malnutrition. Millions lack access to safe water, sanitation, and hygiene services.[56] Sadly, very little, if anything, is said of the Yemeni crisis in the American press. May the only wise God, who vindicated his Christ, hear the cries of his children in Yemen. Maranatha!)

---

[56] "Yemen Crisis." *UNICEF*, www.unicef.org/emergencies/yemen-crisis. Accessed 3 July 2023.

Understanding Irrelevance

When we set out to start a business, a project, a book, or an endeavor of any kind, most of us begin by asking ourselves, who is my audience, and how can I make my work relevant to them? Outside the arena of biblical preaching, these are normal, practical—even necessary—questions. However, for a priest, this line of thinking is inevitably toxic: good for the material well-being of the church but incompatible with the preaching of the biblical story, entrusted part and parcel of the consecrated Lamb placed in your human hands on the day of your ordination.

I can't tell you how often people have reacted to the gospel's content by saying, "That's all fine and good, Father, and I agree, but no one today is interested."

This statement reveals two truths: one, that the person who made it is not studying Scripture, and two, that Scripture itself is again fulfilled because, according to Scripture, no generation is, was, or will ever be interested in Scripture. (I explained previously that no one, let alone the preacher, can agree with or is on the side of Scripture, so I'll leave that point aside.)

Irrelevance is the cornerstone of the biblical genre. I dare say that the mercy of the Scriptural God is that he would pause from his laughter to explain to the human race why he is laughing.

His reason unfolds as the content of Scripture:

Understanding Irrelevance

"A generation goes, and a generation comes…That which has been is that which will be, and that which has been done is that which will be done. So, there is nothing new under the sun." (Ecclesiastes 1:4,9)

Only when we understand what is irrelevant can we devote ourselves to the one genuinely relevant thing.

Grasshoppers

(Homily, Sunday, July 9, 2023)

In the name of the Father, and of the Son, and of the Holy Spirit. Amen.

Christ is in our midst!

Last week, I hinted at an interconnection between the Bible and the Qur'an through the opening of the "womb" in Genesis—the announcement of God's mercy and compassion, repeated in the *bismillah*, which relies on a triliteral root that appears in both Hebrew and Arabic.

I also ridiculed the American pocket-god—the dollar—a criticism picked up in the deacon's homily this morning against human institutions. The expression "pocket-god" is a play on the parable of the *teraphim* in Genesis—the portable gods hidden in Rachel's saddle bag. "Tariff," which means luxury or opulence in Arabic, shares the same triliteral root as the Hebrew *teraphim*. Even in English, the word tariff condemns you.

There may yet be hope for our language.

Listening to Deacon Anthony proclaim the gospel this morning, it struck me that after the demon-possessed came out of the so-called "tombs," the people came out of the city because—from the perspective of the scriptural text, there is no difference between a city and a tomb. Once you build something, you are enslaved by the dynasty of kings, the Pyramid Builders.

Whether you are talking about a city, a temple, a statue, a gravestone, or a house in the suburbs, you are a slave of Egypt, entombed inside a monument to yourself.

The story may say that these men were "coming out of the tombs," but I could just as easily say that the Orthodox were "coming out of the churches" on Pascha, carrying their candles.

Biblical literature is metaphoric.

As I explained last week, the tension in Genesis is between the flesh-and-blood wombs of mothers and the brick-and-mortar dynasties of men. God commands childbirth and childrearing under the authority of his instruction, which liberates the demon-possessed in Matthew's Gospel. In defiance, men build dynasties and grow their kingly legacy by erecting monuments and temples of stone, much like the stone temple we built in lower Manhattan, fashioned after a mother's womb.

Again, in Genesis, Elohim subjugates humanity, limiting the scope of man's dominion to reproduction in the womb. We are temporary. We pass away in each generation. We must not build, and we cannot create, establish, or grow anything. Pharaoh dies, and so do we.

God lives, and he alone provides the seed.

Understanding Irrelevance

It is God who grows children, plants, trees, and other animals in each generation and commands all of us to live together under his rule on land and in the sea. Thus, in Genesis 1-4, we are presented with the generic *ha 'adam*, never to be conflated with the individual *'adam*, whose *toledot* (generations) do not appear until chapter 5. For lack of a better translation, *ha 'adam* refers to humanity as a totality.

An individual human being dies, but we sinfully and arrogantly imagine that humanity as an entity lives and will abide forever. That is why *ha 'adam* is undermined in Genesis 1-4 as the projection of our Platonic ego. The text presents the *toledot*, not of human beings, but of the heavens and the earth, of which the passing, fleeting *ha 'adam*, is itself only a part. There is no "eternal" humanity:

> *"Do you not know? Have you not heard? Has it not been declared to you from the beginning? Have you not understood from the foundations of the earth? It is he who sits above the circle of the earth, and its inhabitants are like grasshoppers, who stretches out the heavens like a curtain and spreads them out like a tent to live in. It is he who reduces rulers to nothing, who makes the judges of the earth meaningless. Scarcely have they been planted, scarcely have they been sown, scarcely has their stock taken root in the earth, but he merely blows on them, and they wither, and the storm carries them away like stubble." (Isaiah 40:21-24)*

From the ungodly perspective of human self-reference, Scripture moves backward, reversing human growth and development from the universal *ha 'adam* of Genesis 1-4 to the individual *'adam* of chapter 5, bringing us back down to earth, to the *'adamah* from which we were formed; to the dust (*'aphar*), from which we were taken—from the facade of opulent stones to weary withering, like fleeting grasshoppers, who wait for Yahweh:

> *"Do you not know? Have you not heard? The everlasting Elohim, Yahweh, the Creator of the ends of the earth does not become weary or tired. His understanding is unsearchable. He gives strength to the weary, and to the one who lacks might he increases power. Though youths grow weary and tired, and vigorous young men stumble badly, yet those who wait for Yahweh will gain new strength; They will mount up with wings like eagles, they will run and not get tired, and they will walk and not become weary." (Isaiah 40:28-31)*

To the everlasting God, the only Creator, who does not grow weary, be the glory, the dominion, and the majesty, always, now and ever, and unto the ages of ages. Amen.

Christ is in our midst!

In the Wilderness

Imagine searching for guidance on the best way to live life. You have the chance to speak with two advisors. The first lifts your spirits. After listening carefully to you, he explains that you have value, possess unique insights, and have something to say and contribute. He argues that your needs and feelings must come first, that everything will work out, and that what matters most is what you want; your life, experiences, and goals count. He provides valuable advice on working diligently, saving wisely, planning strategically, building steadily, establishing, thriving, loving, and relishing a life well-lived, enriched by the company of family, community, friends, children, and grandchildren. He expresses affection, even nostalgia for the person you are, what your shared humanity represents, and who you will become—then you turn to the second advisor.

His name is Paul. He is not interested in what you have to say. He can't hear you; even if he could, he would not listen.[57] Moreover, to make sure that you know, beyond the shadow of any doubt, that nothing of value can ever come from you, as the guest in your home, he ridicules and invalidates your family tree.[58] He explains that you are nothing and have no value as a

---

[57] *"As for you, do not pray for this people, and do not lift up cry or prayer for them, and do not intercede with me; for I do not hear you."* (Jeremiah 7:16)

[58] It was customary in the ancient world for a woman to join a man's patrilineal ancestral line. The *text* of Genesis (preached in Paul's letter to the Ephesians) goes against this custom to uproot human patriarchy, placing it under *Scriptural control* in perpetuity: *"For this reason, a man shall leave his father and his mother and be joined to his wife, and they shall become one flesh."* (Genesis 2:24)

In the Wilderness

husband or a father. You are a tool to be used for a purpose until you are broken and eventually set aside, like a used-up oblation. He admits that this goes against your nature because no man is truly capable of hating his own flesh (Ephesians 5:29), but that's his point; he is giving you a dark saying from Psalm 78; he is hitting you with the painful imposition of the words of Genesis, sealed in the content of his teaching of the Cross in 1 Corinthians: *it is not your life.* There is no such thing as "your" life. It is life, of which human beings are only a small part.

Your plans are not God's plan. The things that you build—your dynasties and eternity projects—offend God. You want to please others, to be surrounded by friends and family, because you want to please yourself. But this is not love. You will not become anything. You are temporary, taken from dust and returning to dust. Like all men, your days are like grass, and the place where you once lived will not remember you. The only thing that stands is the Torah, which was here before you, does not come from you and will be here after you are long gone. As the New Testament explains, there is a chance, after the cancellation of the kings and princes of Israel, that this Torah can be found again in the wilderness, in the arms of the Lamb of God, who is slain for your sake, in cancellation of the Caesars. So, keep your mouth shut and listen to him.[59]

Be honest.

Which advice would you take?

---

[59] Matthew 17:5; Mark 9:7; Luke 9:35

Dark Sayings

You don't have to answer today but believe me:

You *will* have to answer.

A House of Cedar?
(Homily, Sunday, July 16, 2023)

In the name of the Father, and of the Son, and of the Holy Spirit. Amen.

Christ is in our Midst!

These past few years, I have presented a series of homilies with a consistent theme: the destruction of the Temple. Experience has taught me that most people either walk away violently from this teaching or disappear passively, ignoring it. Even those who try to stick around cannot learn, as St. Paul teaches, to hate their own flesh—meaning—their own dynasties. How can we? All of us are interested in our own seed. So, we seal Scripture in a tomb of stone inside our churches, encasing the Gospel of Jesus Christ in a golden prison. St. John Chrysostom thunders:

"This Tabernacle, 'in the wilderness,' was carried about and not locally fixed. He calls it the 'Tabernacle of Witness' of the miracles of the statutes. This is why it and they had no Temple…even then, no Temple! So many wonders and no mention of a Temple! So that although first there is a Tabernacle, yet nowhere a Temple! 'Until the days of David,' he says, and even then, no Temple! 'And he sought to find favor before God,' and did not build! So insignificant a matter was the Temple…they thought Solomon was great, but he was no better than his father, not even shown to be his equal. Thus says the Prophet: 'The Most High does not

dwell in temples made by the hand of man!"" (Homily XVII on Acts vii.)

"Let us learn, therefore, to be strict in life and honor Christ as he desires. To him who is honored, the honor most pleasing is that which he wills, not what we deem best. Peter, too, thought to honor him by forbidding him to wash his feet, but his doing so was not an honor but the contrary. Even so, you must honor him with the honor he ordained: by spending your wealth on poor people, since God has no need at all of golden vessels but of golden souls!" (Homily L on Matthew xiv.)

"If seeing one wrapped in rags and stiff with cold, you should neglect to give him a garment and instead build golden columns, saying you were doing it in his honor, would he not say that you were mocking him and consider it an insult, to the greatest extreme? Let this also be your thought concerning Christ, when he is going about a wanderer, and a stranger, needing a roof to cover him; and you, neglecting to receive him, pour out pavement, and walls, and capitals of columns, and hang up silver chains by means of lamps, but upon him, who is bound in prison, you will not even look." (Homily L on Matthew xiv.)

Beloved in Christ, providentially, today is the forty-day memorial of Kenneth, Jocelyn's grandfather. I asked Jocelyn this morning to remind me of her mother's name, Tamara. It is an important name, and I want to talk about it because Tamar, which shares the same triliteral root in Arabic and Hebrew, is among the most important names in the Old Testament.

Unsurprisingly, Western scholars and theologians, blinded by Victorian morality, "interpret" Tamar's

Dark Sayings

supposed "meaning" rather than submit to its grammatical and literary function.

In the story of Judah, the father of the tribe that produced David's dynasty (an ungodly line forged in stone and destruction, ending in exile) to become pregnant, Tamar was forced to present herself as a prostitute. The woman, Tamar, becomes a mother despite Judah's attempts to obstruct her flesh-and-blood womb.

In Semitic languages, you are born a woman but become a mother only after your womb is opened. As an Arab woman, our own Iman was not considered a reference, a mother, until her womb was opened in childbirth. Only then, she became *Im Khalid*,[60] an almost God-like status in Semitic languages, surpassing *human* patriarchy, because of its functional, and thus, indelible association with moving blood, *damim* (bloods), and thus life, the sole domain of Elohim. Notably, Tamar appears both in the household of Judah and, later, in that of David, God's "beloved."

In 2 Samuel, David, a true master of the game of thrones, waited until after Saul's death to make war against the kingdom of his predecessor:

"Now there was a long war between the house of Saul and the house of David; and David grew steadily stronger, but the house of Saul grew weaker continually." (2 Samuel 3:1)

In David's strategic rise to ascendancy and the consolidation of his power, he dared not move against

---

[60] "Mother of Khalid." In Arabic, *Khalid* means everlasting.

In the Wilderness

Saul before his death. To do so would incur the wrath of God, whose prophet anointed Saul, albeit at the behest of a sinful people. So, David bided his time. Nothing changes under the sun.

The long war in 3:1 never ends. What follows is a tale of betrayal, infighting, murder, cruelty, abuse, opulence, oppression, enslavement, civil war, exile, and, in the broader story of the Bible, failed attempts at reform and restoration.

The storyline of 1 and 2 Samuel, Kings, and Chronicles is a joke. These scrolls catalog the kingdoms of sin as an example of folly for the ages: the game of thrones. A tale of dynasties that collapses into ashes and exile. In the end, they have no children and, despite all their efforts, no legacy of which to speak. These so-called "kings" are an example of what not to do and why what we do now as families, communities, churches, and institutions will never work. Yet, out of their dynastic stench arose Tamar, the godly prostitute, shaming them and exposing their sins "in the name of God, the merciful, the compassionate," binding the warring kingdoms of Judah and Israel in submission, not to David's throne, but to the words of Elohim under the weight of her Hebrew name:

"Palm tree."

In Arabic, Tamar means "date palm,[61]" but in both languages, its function is inescapable: the Palm tree of

---

[61] *"Grieve not, for your Lord has caused a stream of water to flow beneath you. And shake the trunk of this palm tree towards you, it will drop fresh, ripe*

God's oasis in the wilderness, free from the tyranny of king, city, and temple, where the biblical *ro'eh ṣon* (shepherd of flock) finds pasture for his sheep as Elohim's *locum tenens:*

> *"I will feed them in a good pasture, and their grazing ground will be on the mountain heights of Israel. There they will lie down on good grazing ground and feed in rich pasture on the mountains of Israel. 'I will feed my flock, and I will lead them to rest,' declares Adonai Yahweh. I will seek the lost, bring back the scattered, bind up the broken and strengthen the sick; but the fat and the strong I will destroy. I will feed them with judgment." (Ezekiel 34:14-16)*

> *"Then I will set over them one shepherd, my slave David, and he will feed them; he will feed them himself and be their shepherd. And I, Yahweh, will be their Elohim, and my slave David will be prince among them; I Yahweh have spoken." (Ezekiel 34:23–24)*

Even as these mortal kings defiantly schemed and plotted to build their legacy in stone, causing the bloods (*damim*) to spill and run upon the earth, Tamar was working against Judah to give birth in her human flesh, in submission to the will of Yahweh, her Elohim.

That is why Tamar is enshrined at the beginning of the New Testament as a crown jewel in the dynasty of Elohim, the only Patriarch and King, the God and Father of our Lord Jesus Christ, the Good Shepherd, who was sent to the lost sheep of the house (*bayt*) of Israel

---

dates upon you." Mary was consoled and nourished by God after giving birth to Jesus. (Qur'an, Surah Maryam 19:24-25)

In the Wilderness

because he was willing to do what David—and each and every last one of us—will not do: refuse the throne!

God ridicules all of us when he belittles David in 1 Chronicles—especially colonial Americans, the most powerful people on Earth—we who fancy ourselves underdogs fighting against tyranny. Wake up, friends; this is not the eighteenth century. You are not victims fighting an evil king, and you never were—unless you can magically render this homily in the forgotten tongues of one of God's many Algonquian flocks.

During David's "coronation," Elohim does not pronounce him king. Instead, he proclaims: I set you as a shepherd over my people. Your job is to take care of the people, not build a dynasty. He even addresses David as a prince, a subordinate, meaning his *locum tenens*, but not as king:

> *"In times past, even when Saul was king, you were the one who led out and brought in Israel; and Yahweh your Elohim said to you, 'You shall shepherd my people Israel, and you shall be prince over my people Israel.'" (1 Chronicles 11:2)*

There is no god but Elohim!

In 2 Samuel, David goes to Jerusalem, which the text refers to as the city of David. Why would the text of 2 Samuel refer to Jerusalem as the "city of David?" Because your colonial Jerusalem (replete with checkpoints, machine guns, and barbed wire) is not the city of God!

It is not Ezekiel's city of Yahweh, your Elohim! The Lord is *not* there! It is the city of this one who waged war against Saul's house to consolidate his power on the

Dark Sayings

backs of the poor. God sent David to "feed them in a good pasture" on the mountain heights of Israel. David was responsible for feeding the poor, to "seek the lost, bring back the scattered, bind up the broken and strengthen the sick," instead, he fattened himself, claiming a city of stone as his city. He defied Elohim to glorify himself.

Worse, he took the Tabernacle of Witness, assigned by God in Exodus to dwell in the wilderness—as Chrysostom said, "carried about and not locally fixed"—he took it and locked it in the city. He imprisoned it in a tomb, hewn out of the rock by the hand of man in Jerusalem!

In Exodus, the Tabernacle in the Tent of Meeting is iconoclastic. If you do not believe me, take the text of Scripture from Exodus describing the Tent and the Tabernacle and ask an A.I. model to depict it. It cannot. Why? Because Exodus presents you with a Tabernacle, covered by a Tent, in which the Tabernacle covers the Tent, in the wilderness. Beloved in Christ: The Kingdom under the heavens at the end of Matthew's Gospel cannot be depicted, even by George Lucas!

After the exodus from Egypt, you are forced to dwell in the wilderness for forty years until all the generations of the people whom God rescued from bondage to Pharaoh, the Pyramid Builder, have returned to the dust. What is a pyramid? A tomb. A building in which the slaves of the king are buried to worship the bloody tyrant forever and ever. Why do impressive structures like pyramids sit next to the city? To impress and terrify people living in the city, to eliminate all doubt about the temporal king's eternal power.

In the Wilderness

Then came the Good Book to show us the light: the king is a fraud. He will die like any *ben 'adam* and fall like any prince. You fear the wrong gods!

Elohim rescued us from the tomb builders, brought us out into the wilderness, and set us free as his slaves to meet in a Tent that cannot be depicted. An architect cannot draw it. Do you understand my Hebrew? The Tabernacle of Scripture and its Tent of Meeting are unintelligible to Greek Philosophy, civilization, art, and religion and thus indigestible to Plato. You cannot make an icon of the Tent of Meeting, and you cannot dream about it, let alone build it. It has no form!

In the biblical story, the minute David consolidated his power in the "Promised Land," he declared himself a king, claimed a city of stone in his own name, and initiated his dynasty of corruption, in which people like Tamar were abused.

Read Scripture!

There is no king but Elohim!

From the moment Solomon appears, he is already tainted because he cuts a deal with Satan, making an alliance of convenience with Egypt to bring the daughter of Pharaoh into his court:

"Then Solomon formed a marriage alliance with Pharaoh king of Egypt and took Pharaoh's daughter and brought her to the city of David until he had finished building his own house and the house of Yahweh and the wall around Jerusalem." (1 Kings 3:1)

Dark Sayings

Solomon was responsible for God's *bayt* (the household of Yahweh's children), not his *hekal*. Defacto, the wordplay between *bayt* and *hekal* is not functional in translation. Forcefully, in both Arabic and Hebrew, the word *bayt* can refer to a house in one breath and to a household in the next. In a household, a parent raises sons and daughters to God through instruction—not through the fashioning and cutting of stones:

> *"Moreover, I will give you a new heart and put a new spirit within you; and I will remove the heart of stone from your flesh and give you a heart of flesh. I will put my Spirit within you and cause you to walk in my statutes, and you will be careful to observe my ordinances. You will live in the land that I gave to your forefathers, so you will be my people, and I will be your God." (Ezekiel 36:26-28)*

From the beginning, David's rule is tainted by idolatry (stone cutting) because he dabbles in the trappings of pagan ritual in the kingly court. It is unavoidable. You cannot escape it. Power goes to your head. So, God mocks David in 2 Samuel:

> *"Are you the one who should build me a house to dwell in? For I have not dwelt in a house since the day I brought up the sons of Israel from Egypt, even to this day; but I have been moving about in a tent, even in a tabernacle." (2 Samuel 5:5-6)*

In all that time, God explains, when have I ever asked for a house like yours, made of cedar?

Now, for those soft-spoken, family-first Americans living in fat houses with overpriced mortgages in the suburbs ("Harry, Jimmy, Trent, wherever you are out

In the Wilderness

there…"), wipe the smile off your face and remember the words of Haggai (in Arabic, *haj*, "pilgrim," in Hebrew, "my pilgrimages"):

> *"Is it time for you yourselves to dwell in your paneled houses while this house lies desolate? Now, therefore, thus says the Lord of hosts, 'Consider your ways! You have sown much but harvest little; you eat, but there is not enough to be satisfied; you drink, but there is not enough to become drunk; you put on clothing, but no one is warm enough; and he who earns, earns wages to put into a purse with holes.' Thus says the Lord of hosts, 'Consider your ways! Go up to the mountains, bring wood, and rebuild the Temple, that I may be pleased with it and be glorified,' says the Lord." (Haggai 1:4-8)*

Haggai is not a defense of temples but a test of obedience. Is Elohim your reference, or are you here to obey yourself? To obey your thirst? What will you do when the one who destroyed Solomon's Temple asks you to disregard your suburban American home to build *his* Temple only to inform you (as he does in the storyline of Haggai and Zechariah) that he does not need the very Temple he just commanded you to build? With all due respect, who belongs to whom?

You fools!

Read Scripture!

God does not need your bread! There is no reference but Elohim! God is the sole proprietor! He alone is our Father in the heavens, and his Kingdom rules over all! It is God *himself* who provides a house for you within his story, "built" with the *debarim* (words) of his instruction:

Dark Sayings

"Unless Yahweh builds the house, those who build it labor in vain. Unless Yahweh watches over the city, the watchman stays awake in vain." (Psalm 127:1)

In Ezekiel and Isaiah, instead of having land and a capital city with a building constructed by men, Elohim posits himself as the only point of reference for his household, the *bayt ab* (the Father's House), which looks nothing like anything of human construction, let alone the houses we build. Such a Temple can be found nowhere but in our hearing of the prophetic text!

There is no god but Elohim!

God is our shelter and our protection in the wilderness, far away from the things that men build. He alone is our covering and our tent, our Father and provider, if we put our trust in him:

"In my distress I called upon Yahweh; Yahweh answered me and set me in a large place. Yahweh is for me; I will not fear; What can man do to me?" (Psalm 118:5–6)

*"Yahweh is my shepherd, I shall not want. He makes me lie down in green pastures; He leads me beside quiet waters. He restores my soul; He guides me in the paths of righteousness for **his name's sake**." (Psalm 23:1-3)*

"Surely goodness and lovingkindness will follow me all the days of my life, and I will dwell in the house (bayt) of Yahweh forever." (Psalm 23:6)

Yahweh is our Elohim; and we are *his* Temple, *his* body, *his* household, *his* flesh-and-blood children, when we place our trust in his *debarim*, *his* words, and *not* in the work of our own hands:

In the Wilderness

"Their idols are silver and gold, the work of man's hands. They have mouths, but they cannot speak; They have eyes, but they cannot see; They have ears, but they cannot hear; They have noses, but they cannot smell; They have hands, but they cannot feel; They have feet, but they cannot walk; They cannot make a sound with their throat. Those who make them will become like them, everyone who trusts in them." (Psalm 115:4-8)

BELOVED IN CHRIST, the problem is human dynasty: David's, Solomon's, your nation's, your tribe's, the dynasties we build at church through proselytization—the progeny we make for our own glory in God's name, and most importantly, yours: your family's legacy, your opulent suburban homes, your careers, your businesses, your causes, your beliefs, your plans, your woke ideologies, your conservative values, your lust for growth and success, and your love of money. It is all the same thing: you and your children are born of a woman but not born under God's Torah. You are not members of his *bayt*, let alone sheep in his lowly flock.

I want to read something for you this morning to help you understand, once and for all, why we should not speak on a subject unless we know what we are talking about. Too many Christians who know little or nothing about Scripture have too much to say about their personal relationship with the imaginary gods they "form" in their Platonic minds.

Likewise, Christians love to boast about the Protomartyr Stephen—most of all, the Orthodox, who build the most beautiful temples. Yet, despite Stephen's lengthy testimony, few, if any, understand why, instead

Dark Sayings

of feeling "engaged," "uplifted," and "inspired," those upon whose ears his *debarim* fell "were cut to the quick" and "began gnashing their teeth against him." So, in closing, I ask that you listen carefully to Stephen's final words in the Book of Acts:

"'David found favor in God's sight and asked that he might find a dwelling place for the God of Jacob. But it was Solomon who built a house for him. However, the Most High does not dwell in houses made by human hands; as the prophet says:

'THE HEAVENS ARE MY THRONE AND EARTH IS THE FOOTSTOOL OF MY FEET; WHAT KIND OF HOUSE WILL YOU BUILD FOR ME?' SAYS YAHWEH, 'OR WHAT PLACE IS THERE FOR MY REPOSE? 'WAS IT NOT MY HAND WHICH MADE ALL THESE THINGS?'

You men who are stiff-necked and uncircumcised in heart and ears are always resisting the Holy Spirit; you are doing just as your fathers did. Which one of the prophets did your fathers not persecute? They killed those who had previously announced the coming of the Righteous One, whose betrayers and murderers you have now become; you who received the law as ordained by angels, and yet did not keep it.'

Now when they heard this, they were cut to the quick, and they began gnashing their teeth at him. But being full of the Holy Spirit, he gazed intently into heaven and saw the glory (weightiness) *of God, and Jesus standing* (made to stand out as a reference) *at the right hand of God; and he said, 'Behold, I see the heavens opened up and the Son of Man* (a ben 'adam, an ordinary human being, formed from

In the Wilderness

the adamah) *standing at the right hand of God.' But they cried out with a loud voice and covered their ears and rushed at him with one impulse.*

When they had driven him out of the city, (into the wilderness) *they began stoning him; and the witnesses laid aside their robes at the feet of a young man named Saul. They went on stoning Stephen as he called on the Lord and said, 'Lord Jesus, receive my spirit!' Then falling on his knees, he cried out with a loud voice, 'Lord, do not hold this sin against them!' Having said this, he fell asleep." (Acts 7:44-53)*

CHRIST IS RISEN!

"THE WORD THAT CAME TO JEREMIAH FROM THE LORD, saying: 'Stand in the gate of the Lord's house and proclaim there this word and say: Hear the word of the Lord, all you of Judah, who enter by these gates to worship the Lord!

Thus says the Lord of hosts, the God of Israel, 'Amend your ways and your doings, and I will let you dwell in this place. Do not trust in lying words, saying: 'This is the temple of the Lord, the temple of the Lord, the temple of the Lord.'

For if you truly amend your ways and your doings, if you truly practice justice between a man and his neighbor, if you do not oppress the foreigner, the orphan, or the widow, and do not shed innocent blood in this place, nor walk after other gods to your own ruin, then I will let you dwell in this place, in the land that I gave to your fathers forever and ever. Behold, you are trusting in lying words to no avail."

(Jeremiah 7:1-8)

Your Voice

Voices clamor outside the chamber
Witnesses without eyes
Shadows without ears
Words without substance

I listen for your voice
Waiting to be found
It lies hidden beneath a story

I call your name until you beg to stop
Begging the words from above
I become the darkness to enter it

I search for you
I long for you
I listen for your voice

Will I hear you again?

Son of Man

"Truly, truly, I say to you, unless a grain[62] of wheat falls into the earth and dies, it remains alone; but if it dies, it bears much fruit." (John 12:24)

The New Testament storyline emphasizes the question of Jesus's title. The Gospel of Matthew stresses that Jesus is an ordinary *ben 'adam* (Son of Man), while the Gospel of Mark shows him repeatedly demanding that his disciples not tell anyone that he is the Messiah—not because it is a secret—but because of their ignorance of his teaching.

Throughout the gospels, the biblical text is careful not to let the characters in the story or its audience confuse Jesus with a triumphal military or political figure of human strength. Jesus is not a king of his own accord. Nor is he a king by pedigree or election. He is the Suffering Servant in Isaiah, marked by shame, defeat, and humiliation. His kingship is not a foregone conclusion. His only hope is in his Father, hoping against hope that Elohim will remember him *after* the Crucifixion. Only when all hope is "completely cut off" can these dry bones live:

"Then he said to me, 'Son of man, these bones are the entire house of Israel; behold, they say, 'Our bones are dried up, and our hope has perished. We are completely cut off.'[63] Therefore, prophesy and say to them, 'This is what Adonai

---

[62] In Greek *kokkos*, an individual kernel, not to be conflated with *sperma*.

[63] Paul's point of reference for the Greek term *charis* (grace), which Elohim bestows only when all hope of human agency is lost.

Son of Man

Yahweh says: 'Behold, I am going to open your graves and cause you to come up out of your graves, my people; and I will bring you into the land of Israel. Then you will know that I am Yahweh, when I have opened your graves and caused you to come up out of your graves, my people. And I will put my Spirit within you, and you will come to life, and I will place you on your own land. Then you will know that I, Yahweh, have spoken and done it," declares Yahweh.'" (Ezekiel 37:11-14)

Throughout the Bible, the title "Son of God," is associated with characters who grasp at power, like the sons of God in Genesis 6, the arrogant princes and rulers in Psalm 82, or Caesar's inscription[64] in Matthew 22:20. It is only in the Gospel of Luke, after a relentless deprogramming campaign in Matthew and Mark, that the text of the New Testament is willing to bring the titles Son of Man and Son of God together in the biblical storyline.

But *have* we been deprogrammed?

To answer this question, we need only look to history to discover how many emperors, kings, and presidents have painted or still brandish a Cross on their flag or a mere "God bless you" on their lips before marching off to war. How many have twisted the meaning of the gospel into an icon of Jesus with a weapon in his hand?

Either the teaching of the Cross means something, or it doesn't.

---

[64] Hatina, Thomas. *Biblical Interpretation in Early Christian Gospels Volume 1: The Gospel of Mark*. A&C Black, 2006, p. 97.

The Challenge

NYU Chemistry Professor Fired After Students Said His Class Was Too Hard

(Homily, Sunday, October 9, 2022)

In the name of the Father, and of the Son, and of the Holy Spirit. Amen.

Christ is in our midst!

This is going to be a different kind of homily today. I shared this article with all of you this week, and I would like to begin by reading it this morning. I do not know how many people read it, and I do not allow commenting when I post things. That is a didactic stance that will never change. I am not interested in people's feedback, as you well know:

> *"NYU chemistry professor fired after students said his class was too hard.*
>
> *By Robby Soave.*
>
> *(October 3, 2022) Maitland Jones Jr. was a professor of chemistry at Princeton University. In 2007, he semi-retired and began teaching organic chemistry at New York University on an adjunct basis.*
>
> *Not anymore: NYU has fired Jones after students circulated a petition protesting that his class was too hard.*
>
> *But according to Jones, the students weren't putting in enough effort—and had become disengaged, anxious, and indolent as a result of the pandemic.*

Son of Man

'They weren't coming to class, that's for sure,' said Jones. "They weren't watching the videos, and they weren't able to answer the questions."

Jones is profiled in a recent New York Times article that chronicles his firing. The piece also raises uncomfortable questions about elite institutions of higher learning and their utter devotion to appeasing unreasonable student demands. Organic chemistry is the bane of medical students everywhere, precisely because it is such a hard class. But many doctors would argue that that's the point: The class is designed to act as an effective gatekeeper, preventing underqualified students from entering the field of medicine.

'This article made my skin crawl,' tweeted Alice Dreger, a bioethicist and former professor of medical humanities. 'We aren't going to end up with good doctors by letting undergrad pre-meds pass organic chem because universities want to protect their US News rankings.'

According to The New York Times, 82 of Jones' 350 students signed the petition last spring; it alleged that too many of them were failing and that this was unacceptable. The students cited emotional and mental health complaints to make the case that Jones ought to make the class less difficult.

'We urge you to realize that a class with such a high percentage of withdrawals and low grades has failed to make students' learning and well-being a priority and reflects poorly on the chemistry department as well as the institution as a whole,' the petition read.

The Times article suggests that throughout the pandemic, Jones made a number of accommodations for struggling

Dark Sayings

students. He reduced the difficulty of his exams, but students were still failing them.

'Students were misreading exam questions at an astonishing rate,' said Jones.

The article does note that the petition never called for Jones to be fired. But the university evidently decided that the best way to resolve the situation was to turn him loose.

His departure is certainly a loss for NYU's academic caliber. After all, Jones is a lion in the field of organic chemistry, publishing 225 papers in his 40-year career. He literally wrote the textbook, "Organic Chemistry," which weighs in at 1,300 pages.

'[Jones] learned to teach during a time when the goal was to teach at a very high and rigorous level,' Paramjit Arora, a professor of chemistry at NYU and former colleague of Jones told The Times. 'We hope that students will see that putting them through that rigor is doing them good.'

NYU clearly feels differently about the matter.

'NYU had in Professor Maitland Jones a faculty member with a one-year appointment specifically to teach organic chemistry,' wrote John Beckman, a spokesperson for NYU, in a statement to Reason. 'In one of his organic chemistry classes in the spring 2022 there were, among other troubling indicators, a very high rate of student withdrawals, a student petition signed by 82 students, course evaluations scores that were by far the worst not only among members of the Chemistry Department but among all the University's undergraduate science courses, and multiple student

Son of Man

complaints about his dismissiveness, unresponsiveness, condescension, and opacity about grading.'

Beckman continued:

So, what exactly would be the argument for renewal of this appointment? NYU has lots of hard courses and lots of tough graders among the faculty - they don't end up with outcomes like this. Surely, among the many things a university should stand up for - including academic freedom, academic rigor, and a robust research enterprise - one of them should be good teaching. Good teaching shouldn't be pitted against rigor as an excuse for poor teaching; good teaching and rigor are perfectly compatible, and the latter is not a threat to the former at NYU.

But the question isn't whether students deserve good teachers—of course, they do—but whether good teachers should feel compelled to pass students who fail to demonstrate mastery of an extraordinarily important and complex subject matter.

'Celebrated organic chemistry professor Maitland Jones Jr. had high standards, and we can't have that in 2022," writes the leftist author and teacher Freddie deBoer. "NYU students—who are, by any rational measure, some of the most privileged people on planet earth—organized a petition and got him fired. I hope you never get treated by one of the doctors who emerges from this mess."'[65]

---

[65] Soave, Robby. "NYU Chemistry Professor Fired After Students Said His Class Was Too Hard." *Reason.com*, 4 Oct. 2022, reason.com/2022/10/03/maitland-jones-jr-organic-chemistry-nyu-fired.

Dark Sayings

That article, for me, says it all. It characterizes, as far as I'm concerned, what I'm about as a priest. I always try to guess how many years I've been a priest. It's a running joke. It will be twenty years this year, and I would like to take the opportunity to speak with you for a few minutes about where we are as a parish.

When we moved into this building, we got the renovation done in three and a half weeks—three and a half weeks—and I'm certain that most of you still don't know why I was in such a hurry. I'm going to tell you why right now. It's very simple. It's because from the day I was ordained until today, I have preached two things. Number one, that people should read the Bible, and number two, that at the heart of the teaching of Scripture is the destruction of the Temple.

The Temple is the problem.

So, when we got here, I wanted to make sure that the one thing that was the biggest threat to my ministry—this building—would be immediately and as quickly as possible dispensed with as an obstacle. I didn't want one single meeting to discuss anything about the building.

Just get it done.

So, I used all my powers, experience, intellect, and capabilities, which I have in spades, to push forward and spend the money to get us up and running in three weeks. And I had help from other capable people.[66]

---

[66] My cousin, James Yacoub, who acted as General Manager, and my maternal uncle, George Kanavati. In my dad's absence, my

Son of Man

And it was done.

It was done so fast that people were frustrated. Some had plans for what they wanted to do and were frustrated that it got done so quickly. But I wanted to confuse and frustrate their plans because I had one plan.

I have always had one plan.

And if I ask you what that one plan was, and still is, some of you might answer—but I'm still not sure, even if you say the words, that you are on the same page as me.

God doesn't need me.
He doesn't need you.
He certainly does not need our building.

We need his teaching.
We are here to study Scripture.

I have said it so consistently. I mean, the first thing we did, and people were frustrated when they had plans for carpets, and kitchens, and stoves—I don't know what people were thinking about—ceilings—and the first thing I did was put a sign on the front of the building saying, God has no interest in our building; this is not his house; I remember the look of disdain people had that I would waste time making a sign saying, God doesn't want our building. But I was desperate to make sure everyone understood: We need to get this part out

---

uncle George formally extended my grandfather's blessing. This holds special value in the Middle East since the maternal uncle is regarded as paternal to all one's offspring.

Dark Sayings

of the way so we can sit down together and continue Bible study.

But somehow, and I think the Pandemic forced the question (the Pandemic was a great blessing in this sense), everyone came to church wanting something else. It was always evident to me, but the Pandemic exposed it.

Because, you know, and as you recall, coming out of the Pandemic, I pushed, and I pushed, and I pushed, and I pushed the question of biblical nihilism in my preaching. Nothing matters; nothing means anything; none of this has any purpose "under the sun."

I pushed that question to the ultimate limit that Scripture pushes it. A great many people coming to St. Elizabeth's at that time had already decided, "What's the point?" I don't get why we're doing it, and those of you still showing up for reasons other than Scripture started to ask, "What's the point?" Why am I supporting you, Father Marc? Why am I supporting the community? Why should I?

That question, "What's the point," which Scripture forces you to deal with, which the Pandemic thrust upon many people in the last two years, is why everyone in this country is quitting; and it is a really crappy question, an extremely sinful question.

That's why many of you were projecting it on me: "Is Father Marc going to quit? Does Father Marc hate the priesthood? Father Marc should quit. Father Marc doesn't want to be a priest. Maybe he's sick of it." I'm not sick of it. I've been going to Vespers since I was ten years old. If none of you show up, I'll keep chanting. I like it, but that's not why I'm here. I'm not going to quit. Even if I hated it, I would never quit because I know why I'm here.

When you ask the question, "What's the point?" When you say, "Maybe Father Marc wants to quit," it exposes your sin: you are still asking what's in it for you. How can *I* be fulfilled?

"As for man, his days are like grass; Like a flower of the field, so he flourishes. When the wind has passed over it, it is gone, and its place no longer knows about it." (Psalm 103:15-16)

I have been reading those verses since I was ten years old, in *this* neighborhood, walking to church. Why would I stop reading them now? Why would I stop trusting in those verses?

Since I was Sebastian's age, I have known there is nothing in it for me. Your problem is that you still think there's something in it for you. That's why you can't figure out what the point is.

We are here if we accept the proposition of Scripture, which you *don't* have to accept. That's the choice you have. If we accept it, the Lord commands us to obey his teaching, study it, and search it.

I invited the Parish Council to breakfast this year because they were still discussing buildings and budgets, five-year plans, mammon, and all kinds of nonsense. And I wanted to appeal to them once more to become my fellow workers, my co-laborers in God's vineyard. I wanted to ask them to join me in preaching the gospel.

Dark Sayings

Like any household, we have to do administration and all this other crap, but it's secondary. We are here primarily to study Scripture and must be serious about it. Now, I want to remind all of you of what I told you for twenty years, half of which (for ten years) I did not receive a dime for my priestly service.

For twenty years, I've been saying that we are here to read the Bible, and God doesn't need us. He doesn't need our building, and *the central teaching of Scripture* is the destruction of the Temple, the destruction of Jesus Christ. I have preached those words even when I didn't fully understand their implication.

I've said it for twenty years, and some of the people on the council were my students in church school when they were a little older than Sebastian.

I went to the Parish Council that morning to share ideas from a book I'm working on. But the council just wanted to talk about money and buildings, and I said, "Well, there it is." Of course, the book I'm writing is about surviving as a parish in the wilderness as God's flock, which is how I was fortunate to grow up, and not as a brick-and-mortar institution. This is a different way of thinking about church life: subsistence living in the wilderness of the biblical text. Being minimalist: just enough of an institution that we can function as a parish and continue to do the real work, which has nothing to do with growth, buildings, councils, meetings, processes, budgets, and other such nonsense.

In other words, *God's house*, not our building.

Take my aunt Yvonne, who found life in our Bedouin camp. I don't want to trade that life for, you know, forms and documents and processes and budgets. I'm not interested. I have worked a corporate job for as long as I have been alive. I'm not here to sell anything. I'm interested in the Shepherd's Voice, which isn't mine and is not for sale! It's the voice of the biblical text!

So, I sat there at the Parish Council (and you all know that I was under tremendous stress in my personal life at the time) trying to reason with them—and in the midst of all this, someone used this ungodly phrase:

"The legacy of the building."

They talked about the *legacy of the building!* It was a profound betrayal. At that point, I could not abide. It was a matter of duty. Most of you think I am crazy, but there is this powerful saying by St. Anthony the Great that I want to mention right now. It's an old saying, from the *Apophthegmata*:

"A time is coming when men will go insane, and when they see someone who is not insane, they will attack him, saying, 'You are insane; you are not like us.'"

I'm sure that most people thought I was going crazy, and you often think I am crazy, but I'm not crazy. I could not sit at table with people who were going to talk about the *legacy of a building*. I *had* to break communion with that discussion.

That discussion was not sustainable for me.

So, I walked out, and what troubled me was that I knew that no one understood why I walked away. After twenty years of me saying we are here to study Scripture and God doesn't need our building, it's a real head-

Dark Sayings

scratcher that no one understood why I walked out of that meeting.

For me, it's a head-scratcher because I'm a clear speaker. No one ever hears me speak and says, what did he say? People may not like what I say, but people know exactly what I say, which means it's not a question of comprehension but of disobedience. But as God told Samuel, it's not personal. It's not a question of people not respecting or loving the messenger. As the Good Book says, it's not between you and me. It's between you and the God of Scripture.

The legacy of the building? Really?

So, it was a challenge and proposition to the council and each of you, and it stands today. I'm not angry or frustrated and have no right to be.

I love this parish. I love this neighborhood. I love this church. I love being a priest, and the invitation remains for each of you to be my coworkers, but to be coworkers means that you must accept that we're not building anything and we're not going anywhere. And if we act according to Scripture, we will be invisible, and we will be disrespected, and we will be shunned and laughed at. We will be disregarded and abandoned. We will not grow. We won't be a shining example of what a great parish is. If we are, then we have sinned and gone astray.

The Pandemic was a *kairos*.[67]

---

[67] An opportunity presented by God to initiate an action at a time *he* considers favorable. A chance to submit to *his will* at a passing

Son of Man

The difficulties in my family were a great blessing because they pushed me to put the teaching to the test personally and to accept that I have no control over anything, that I am in the hands of the terrible and terrifying God, and that I must be willing to lose everything: my family, the parish, my job, *everything*. Those who were close to me can bear witness to this because they saw it. I was willing to lose everything but to keep standing firm in the commandment, whatever the cost.

As a colleague and someone I love dearly recently said, I'm an anachronism. Martin confirmed it on a recent trip to Chicago. A man out of time, a Roman patrician, and I won't change. I'm a Bedouin *sheikh*. You all see how I serve liturgy and preach; you know how I operate. I am not interested and will not change; this is not a popularity contest, but whatever I am, I'm your priest.

So, I want to share a few quotes with you today and reissue a challenge. I'm going to speak out of character because these are mostly worldly quotes. I'm going back to the beginning of this conversation, but I will speak as a fool,[68] as Paul would say, a turn of phrase I love to borrow.

I love the language that St. Paul gives us, allowing us to step out of character and speak in worldly terms. A way to appeal to your insanity as people who are not

---

moment of *his* choosing.; "The time (*kairos*) is fulfilled, and the kingdom of God is at hand; repent and trust (*pisteuete*) in the gospel." (Mark 1:15)

[68] 2 Corinthians 11:1,23

Dark Sayings

scriptural begging you to understand what I am saying scripturally to you. I am appealing to you to go back to the beginning, to start over, and decide once again to face the question posed to you in Deuteronomy, to submit to God. So, I'm just going to share some secular quotes with you:

> *"We choose to go to the moon in this decade and to do the other things, not because they are easy, but because they are hard because that goal will serve to organize and measure the best of our energies and skills. Because that challenge is one that we are willing to accept. One that we are unwilling to postpone." (John F. Kennedy)*

> *"It is our choices that show what we truly are, far more than our abilities. For you, for me, people who are living in Western society. People who are not repressed, who are free. We can choose. You've got to work. It's about structure. It's about discipline. It's all these deadly things that your schoolteacher told you you needed." (J. K. Rowling)*

Of course, this one you'll recognize:

> *"Nothing will work unless you do." (Maya Angelou)*

This last one we used to have on T-shirts at St. Elizabeth's:

> *"Work, pray, and hope." (St. Elizabeth)*

St. Elizabeth's as a parish has always been about work. Not festivals, dinners, projects, fundraisers, busy work, and all that nonsense. For Christ's sake. Who cares? Look, I want to explain the scandal to you. We have in our church the personal library of Father Paul Tarazi.

Son of Man

We just did a Bible study on Samuel. Did anyone read any of the commentaries on Samuel from that library? Has anyone checked out a book from that library? Is anyone doing any work?

"Oh, we're not scholars, Father Marc."

Well, what did J.K. Rowling say?

"It's our choices that show what we truly are far more than our abilities."

Do you really think that this is about talent and ability? Do you think that's what this is? Where do you think I come from? Do you think it's because I'm talented? Do you think I was the best student at seminary? If that's what you think, you're a fool. It's about time, pressure, and effort.

The reason I teach as a priest the way this beautiful man, Maitland Jones, teaches organic chemistry is because I think that every single one of you, every last one of you, including my mother, who says that she's not capable—I think that every last one of you, beginning with my own mother, is capable, and that's why I never give up fighting.

That is why I have personally confronted each of you over the last twenty years, and every one of you has a reason to be angry or frustrated with me. Every single one of you has been injured or offended by me somehow at some point because I think it's worth it.

That is *my* statement.

Dark Sayings

I am a Roman patrician.[69] I am not the Shepherd, but in the spirit of image (*selem*) in Hebrew, as Father Paul has explained in his most recent books, I am the Shepherd's shadowy reflection, a functional representative, put in place to recite the Psalms for you, and that's what I will do in Byzantine chant until I drop.

So, my sincere hope and prayer in this special homily is that you would go back, each and every one of you, and reconsider the one time you could make a choice, in Baptism, whether or not to accept the Bible as your reality, and the Scriptural God as your authority.

The church is not a "safe space" to feel good. It is a place to be criticized and judged by Scripture, to be challenged to "change your ways and your doings," as it says on the door. If you accept that challenge, and most importantly, if you accept the premise that it's not about

---

[69] The pastor's challenge is to transport those hearing the words of Scripture back to the historical, linguistic, and geographical reality of the historical audience of the text. The scope of this audience is narrow and distant, making the task arduous. Consider the vast distance between you and your children or your parents, living in the same society, separated only by a few years, speaking the same language. Paul wrote individual letters to the Galatians, the Romans, the Corinthians, etc., to address specific issues to people living in specific times and places millennia ago. The Bible was not written to a general or universal audience. You cannot make it relevant for you today. Any attempts to do so unlock new forms of idolatry, for example, "reception history." Instead, the teacher's task is to make the Roman household of Paul's letters functional in the minds of his parishioners so that they can go back in time and hear what Paul said once, long ago, in order to deal with a specific problem. Can we learn from how Paul handled his pastoral challenges? I hope so.

you, and you set aside once and for all this sinful question, "What's the point?" If you accept that the institution is a dead end and that it is empty; if you accept this and that there's nothing in it for you—if you go against your biology, which wants to ascend and achieve and grow—if you set this aside, that your fleshly, humanistic understanding of salvation, which is worldly and anti-scriptural, is about achievement—if you can learn to let go of that and be baptized into Jesus Christ—for me, those words hold so much power:

"As many as have been baptized into Jesus Christ have put on Christ." (Galatian 3:27)

If you are willing to submit to this teaching of St. Paul, please, by all means, I encourage you, I challenge you, I don't know what the word is, I *exhort you* to keep coming to church and to make everything you do about Scripture, and by no means, in a shallow way.

When the Parish Council meets, take thirty minutes and study the Bible first before taking up administrative tasks. Don't do as the Gentiles do and say, "Well, Father's value is to talk about the Bible, and my value is to talk about money. My value is to talk about this. My value, my value, my value…" There is no value! The only value is Scripture! So, learn it and become valuable because Scripture is valuable. Learn Scripture and teach it. That is the only gift. There are no other gifts. Because friends, the need is great. There is nothing in it except love for others and the generation not yet born.

To God alone be the glory, the dominion, and the majesty always now and ever and to ages of ages. Amen.

Christ is in our midst!

*"Halt, my two friends, and we will weep
over the memories of a beloved
   And a campsite that was at the sand dune's rim,
between al-Dakhūl and Ḥawmal
   And Tūḍiḥ and al-Miqrāt, whose traces
have not been effaced by the weaving
   of the north and south winds."*

—*Imru' al-Qays*[70]

---

[70] Al-Qays', the father of Arabic poetry, employs "the emotionally evocative *nasib*, and the metaphor of place" to express feelings of desolation, human transience, and loss.; Elinson, Alexander. *Looking Back at al-Andalus: The Poetics of Loss and Nostalgia in Medieval Arabic and Hebrew Literature.* Brill, 2009, p. 17.

Stand Your Ground

"Lord, now lettest thou thy servant depart in peace,
 according to thy word:
For mine eyes have seen thy salvation,
Which thou hast prepared before the face of all people;
A light to lighten the Gentiles, and the glory of thy people Israel."
 —St. Simeon's Prayer (Luke 2:29-32)

Scripture is clever. When Simeon stands in the temple waiting, he does so at the pleasure of his master. He has no agency, control, or personal expectations, yet he has a duty. As his very name suggests, he is to hear and obey the words of God until his death, trusting that God will fulfill his promise to achieve salvation, carrying those words in victory over the nations. He has no right to insist on an outcome and, at the same time, no right to lose hope. So, what was Simeon's job? What is a man with no agency supposed to do?

David said:

"Those who trust in the Lord are like Mount Zion, which cannot be shaken but abides forever. As the mountains surround Jerusalem, so the Lord surrounds his people both now and forever." (Psalm 125:1-2)

Moses said to the people:

"Do not be afraid! Stand firm and see the salvation of the Lord, which he will accomplish for you today; for the Egyptians whom you see today, you will never see again, forever. The Lord will fight for you while you keep silent." (Exodus 14:13-14)

Stand Your Ground

Stand firm. Stand your ground. Hear and obey. Trust in the words of Scripture. Stay the course–each person in that state in which he was called.

It's not that a person of duty does not have agency. On the contrary, such a person transfers agency to their allegiance. They still have work to do. The literary metaphor of Simeon standing firm at his post reflects such work, which defers all agency to the commandments of God.

Standing firm in anticipation of a great war with no hope of victory and trusting in God for salvation to the point of death is hardly standing still. On the contrary, it's frightening, challenging, and—as the story goes— honorable and breathtaking.

In Memory of Daniel del Castillo

(Eulogy, Saturday, June 8, 2019)

In the name of the Father, and of the Son, and of the Holy Spirit. Amen.

Christ is in our midst!

To Daniel's[71] beloved wife, Renae, and his mother, Marcia; To Renae's mother Claudette, and her family; To his sisters, Deborah and Michele; To Giovanni,

---

[71] The Lord's House is built out of his story at work in daily life for the sake of his sons and daughters. Such people, like Daniel, are members of his Body, offspring in his *toledot*, not made by human hands. Daniel and I sojourned together for a time in our Refugee Church on St. Paul's West Side.

Dark Sayings

Alessandro, Isabella, Cezanne and Hudson, and to the least of these, our dearest Hayden: Christ is in our midst!

All of us live with fear. We fear the power that others hold over us; we fear loss; we fear the future; these fears drive us to seek security, almost always, at the expense of the misunderstood other. Sometimes, we are so afraid that we build walls to protect ourselves from them.

The novelty of Daniel del Castillo, a man so valued in his service to the United States, is that his wisdom came from the very people and places we fear. The cultures that animated Daniel's intellect were the fragments of fallen societies, of once-great civilizations—places where he was able to live and work. This was Daniel's great fortune since he was under no illusions of permanence.

Scripture itself is an invitation to understand everything from the perspective of the end. This knowledge replaces fear with certainty: that all things are vanity; (Ecclesiastes 1:2) that human power and prestige are passing away; that all men die, and in the end, all nations fail.

For those who accept it, this knowledge instills clarity of purpose, emboldening its adherents to speak and act fearlessly, standing outside of history, in service of the common good.

In the biblical Book of Daniel, we are confronted with the scope of human history, from the Babylonian Empire until the end of days, measured by the rise and fall of empires. Through the twists and turns of humanity's perpetual instability and cruelty, in the Book of Daniel, it is the Lord's teaching that remains constant.

Stand Your Ground

It is the Lord's teaching that brought honor to the prophet Daniel in the midst of Nebuchadnezzar's court.

It is the Lord's teaching, handed down to the Three Youths, that set them free from tyranny, giving them the courage to walk about "in the midst of the flames without harm." (Daniel 3:25)

It is the Lord's teaching that offers the same freedom to every generation.

From age to age, the God of the Book of Daniel sends his prophet to speak on his behalf in the king's court; to bear witness to his teaching in the midst of "the lion's den." (Daniel 6:16)

We do not know how the Prophet Daniel and the Three Youths ended up in this court; but we do know the path of our beloved Daniel del Castillo.

We know and remember Daniel as an erudite and soft-spoken man, who conveyed a fierce truth with love.

This version of Daniel would not have been possible were it not for the formidable voice of his childhood truth-tellers, a precarious community of refugees and immigrants who spoke fiercely and lovingly, with no regard for consequence.

Daniel and I were brought up together in what he called our "tight-knit, micro-community," a small, scrappy immigrant church on St. Paul's West Side, a poor neighborhood, host to waves of immigrants of many religions and ethnicities; a place where Jewish and Arab immigrants embraced each other genuinely and lovingly. In this setting, the church of our youth, now burned to the ground, was the cornerstone of a once-thriving inner-city Arab-Christian neighborhood.

At the center of this community served our beloved priest and my grandfather, Father Essa Kanavati, a Palestinian refugee and a towering father figure in Daniel's life. A man, who like all those before him, preached fiercely in defense of the love of neighbor against the love of money, which he understood as the Achilles' heel of his new homeland. He was not wrong.

There were other voices present there, like that of my father, Paul, an Egyptian man whom Daniel once called "a formidable figure [and] a luminary" whose legacy, in Daniel's words, "still lingers."

Like the voice of Daniel's godfather, my Uncle Louie, whose commitment to education played a central and formative role in Daniel's career as a writer, which began in his twenties, when he himself created educational programs for the Minnesota Humanities Commission.

Daniel and I grew up listening to our dads and my uncles arguing passionately and vociferously about politics, society, and religion. These were important confrontations of immeasurable value because they opened our minds to the world of ideas.

"By the very act of arguing," C.S. Lewis wrote, "you awake the patient's reason, and once it is awake, who can foresee the result?"

There were other voices still: that of his godmother, my aunt Vickie, and of his beloved mother, Marcia, a daughter of Lebanon, who, more than anyone, opened

Stand Your Ground

Daniel's mind to the literature, history, and intellectual life of the Middle East.

As a boy, Daniel used to wait eagerly for his father of Mexican descent, Daniel Sr., to come home from work. Daniel Jr. was always ready to go someplace, to be on the move. Anytime Deb would go for a bike ride, Daniel would hurriedly get ready, grab his bike, and rush to keep up with his big sister. Even as a boy, he seemed to understand that life's transience demanded action.

They rode their bikes through the old neighborhood, in the seventies and eighties, a place made of the same stuff as Daniel. They must have passed Morgan's Mexican-Lebanese Deli a thousand times. Just one block from the old church, Morgan's too, is now gone.

Bike-riding was replaced with intellectual exchange, as Daniel tagged along with Deb to the Walker Art Center, the Minneapolis Institute of Art, the ballet, the Guthrie Theater, and countless academic meetings on social issues, the Middle East, politics, and race.

Daniel was a curious child surrounded by books. Like so many thinkers who came of age in the seventies and eighties, he felt a deep sense of alienation from the culture, a sentiment amplified by the color of his skin. This alienation drew him closer to societies and ideas often dismissed, if not despised, by the American mainstream. Societies where the truth—that all men die and all nations fail—need not be explained.

His parents' library contained ethnographies, liturgical texts, great works in sociology, books of poetry and theology, and a diverse collection of literary works favoring no single culture.

Dark Sayings

Bertrand Russel, Khalil Gibran, Erich Fromm, Franz Kafka, Edward Said, and other giants contributed to an early intellectual life that pointed outward and eastward. Art was also an important component of Daniel's formation. It began with the Levantine iconography of our childhood church but came into focus with Marcia's emphasis on aesthetics.

Always a writer, a precocious Daniel used to recount the evening news for his mother and sisters, retelling stories from different perspectives. He was captivated by the power of sharing information in order to educate. Later, as a photographer and writer, he brought the perspective of the outcast and the misunderstood other to the center of his work.

At university, Daniel mastered the Arabic language, discovering the music of Um Kalthoum and the poems of Kabbani, Al Muttanabbi, and Mahmoud Darwish, which he could recite by memory:

> *"Words sprout like grass from the prophetic mouth of Isaiah: 'If you won't believe now, you'll never believe.' I walk as if I were someone else. My wound is a white rose of the gospels. My hands are two pigeons hovering around a cross carrying the weight of the earth." – Mahmoud Darwish*

These verses, of exile and suffering, heightened Daniel's moral sensibilities and focused his life-long priorities. When he, Deb, Giovanni, and Alessandro traveled through southern Lebanon, Daniel photographed the bullet-ridden towns and places of massacre. He trusted the conscience of his audience—anyone willing to look—to see the truth of the misunderstood other in his photos.

Stand Your Ground

This pattern in Daniel's work, of seeking out the unheard, drew strength from his childhood truth-tellers, who spoke clearly and fearlessly.

At the Minnesota Humanities Commission, for the first time, Daniel's alienation was transformed into purpose, when he stood up for a friend whose skin color and accent drew mistreatment. Faced with an uncomfortable racism often disguised as "Minnesota nice," he challenged colleagues to broaden their perspectives in the same way the refugee and immigrant truth-tellers in his life challenged each other.

Daniel secretly sent a letter to the Commission, typewritten on letterhead of the Palestinian Liberation Organization, inviting the Commission to collaborate with Palestinian institutions.

They were terrified, but Daniel was satisfied. The letter had exposed a truth, that racism is fueled by our fear of what might happen to us and of what might be lost if we open ourselves to the misunderstood other.

It is fear that builds walls and alienates us from each other, it is fear that tears down bridges.

It must have been hard for Daniel to admit that it was a prank. Still, the letterhead was authentic, one of many treasures gathered from his travels.

When the king sought the death of Babylon's would-be soothsayers, it was Daniel, the mighty prophet, who took courage from the Lord's wisdom to confront the captain of the king's guard:

Dark Sayings

"Do not destroy the wise men of Babylon," he exclaimed, "Take me into the king's presence, and I will declare the interpretation to the king!" (Daniel 2:24)

In similar fashion, our Daniel always spoke up in those moments that mattered most, never cowering from an opportunity to speak the truth, no matter the risk. From his early years in Egypt and Lebanon to more recent endeavors in Afghanistan and Iraq, Daniel was fearless in seeking the truth and speaking it with disciplined clarity.

In the book of Daniel, when the king threatened to murder the Three Youths for refusing to worship his gods, they were fearless—even defiant—in their response. They explained to the king, that it was their God, not the king, who had the power to save or destroy them, and they were willing to take this stand, even if God himself chose not to intervene on their behalf. (Daniel 3:18)

It is the end that clarifies. It is the end that creates wisdom, granting youth the experience of age. It is knowledge of the end that quiets our fears, giving us courage to stand in the face of tyranny.

These men did not fear the king, because they knew that everything comes to an end, including themselves, including the king, including Babylon. Their fealty was not to a man, but to a teaching. They knew that what endures is the wisdom of God that safeguards life in the midst of the flames of tyranny, from age to age. Knowing this end gave our Daniel courage, direction, and purpose in these worrisome times. His death affords each of us the same opportunity.

Stand Your Ground

In Afghanistan, Daniel's journalism came at the risk of his own life. He entered the country on September 10, 2001 in pursuit of a story on education under the Taliban. He was able to interview two Afghan scholars at Kabul University before his trip was cut short by the fateful events of September 11. At once, his life was in danger.

Daniel did not have permission to leave the country, and the Taliban were in no mood to accommodate. Were it not for his minder, who risked his life to warn him, Daniel may have been imprisoned or worse. This brave man helped disguise Daniel as a member of the Taliban and daringly smuggled him out of the country. As an advocate for the marginalized, it bothered Daniel that his work put someone else in danger. In later years, Daniel expressed regret at not knowing the outcome of his friend's life. He could never live comfortably knowing how this man and countless others in the Middle East lived so precariously.

During his years in Lebanon, Daniel wrote for The Daily Star, the famous English language newspaper headquartered in Beirut.

His articles told stories to educate and build bridges in Lebanon's post civil war era. Daniel understood the pain of alienation that came from his own life. Instead of wallowing, he sought to heal the wounds of isolation afflicting the misunderstood other.

He conducted personal interviews with pivotal figures of the Middle East, among them, Hasan Nasrallah, Walid Jumblatt, and Hanan Ashrawi.

Dark Sayings

He wrote about politics and religion, in Lebanon, topics that are inseparable. Daniel was a Greek Orthodox who sojourned in the minority Druze community. He spent time in their villages and sacred spaces. He embraced the Druze people with a spirit of humility and a genuine desire to understand. Perhaps that's why Jumblatt was so open to speaking with him—our Daniel—the marginalized boy who served at the altar with Father Kanavati in his precarious but scrappy micro-community.

"Love," Dr. King wrote, "is not this sentimental something that we talk about. It's not merely an emotional something. Love is creative, understanding goodwill for all men."

"It is love that will save our world and our civilization, love, even [and especially] for [our] enemies."

Our Daniel, the builder of bridges, sought human connection for all of us—across all manmade boundaries. Our Daniel, a man who would be summoned to advise generals and presidents.

Daniel's first exposure to government service was in Iraq, where he interpreted—not dreams—but the Iraqi press for the local ambassador. Later, as a Foreign Service Officer, he would travel the world. More than once during his career, Daniel was requested "by-name," for dangerous assignments to fill difficult and sensitive diplomatic posts, a rare and significant honor in the U.S. Military.

During his tour of duty in Nepal, an American boy went missing. In despair, the young man's parents reached out to former Vice President Walter Mondale

Stand Your Ground

with a simple request, "Please, help us." Mr. Mondale called Daniel.

It was difficult, but with a perseverance he learned from my grandfather, Daniel found their son. The boy had died while hiking alone in the mountains. Daniel wrote a heartfelt letter, comforting the parents in the face of immeasurable sorrow.

"What I remember best about Daniel," a colleague wrote, was his ability "to reach out to the parents and families of American citizens involved in…our most tragic cases and…to say just the right thing to let them know he felt their loss deeply and would do all that he could to help. He made many people feel just a little bit better at what must have been the worst [hour] of their [life]."

"Even in the inevitable moments," King wrote, "when all seems hopeless, men know that without hope, they cannot really live, and in agonizing desperation, they cry for the Bread of Hope."

The Bread of Life: the teaching of a Crucified King, who instead of consuming his subjects (Micah 3:3) is consumed by them. (1 Corinthians 11:24)

Daniel was in Stuttgart, Germany, when he was ordered to report to the White House under the administration of President Barak Obama, to be the Director of East African Affairs on the staff of the National Security Council. Later, he was assigned to the office of the Secretary of State. The details of Daniel's service during these years are unknown to us. One thing we do know, Daniel had a parking space at the White House.

Dark Sayings

As Daniel's colleague in the Foreign Service, Dan Hamilton, explained, "The stories about this guy go on, and on, and on, and on."

"Daniel," he confided, "always, always remembered his family and the community from where he came, and remembered that everything he did…he did in their names and on their behalf. We will always, always remember him and the principles he embodied."

"The community from where he came"—made up of refugees and immigrants from places often dismissed, if not feared, by the American mainstream—a church community judged by God, burned to the ground, and long gone. A reminder of what Daniel knew to be true: that all things are vanity; all things are passing away, and all men die. It is this truth that gave him courage, direction, and purpose in these worrisome times. Daniel, too, is now gone. All that remains is the teaching he received; the teaching that sustained him; the hope for the next generation.

For as long as I can remember, Daniel was the one person in the room you could count on to say the thing that needed to be said, no matter how uncomfortable the situation. In this sense, he reminded me of my dad. No conjecture, just analysis based on facts and the courage to speak it, no matter the rank of dissenting voices. That is exactly how he conducted himself as a Foreign Service Officer. His fealty, Mr. Hamilton explained, was not to a man, but to his oath, to uphold the law of the land.

Daniel knew that evil—the product of human fear—was real. This knowledge amplified the biblical and prophetic voice always at work on his conscience—in the face of unthinkable moral dilemmas—always prodding him and renewing his mind in the service of "that which is good and acceptable and perfect" in the sight of the Lord. (Romans 12:2)

In this sense, Daniel was a double agent: a citizen of the coming Kingdom who found himself working inside the government of the present one. (Galatians 1:4)

"The God of heaven," proclaimed Daniel to the king, "will set up a Kingdom which will never be destroyed, and that kingdom will not be left for another people; it will crush and put an end to all these kingdoms, but it will itself endure forever." (Daniel 2:44)

Deb recalls the day that Daniel left for Egypt to study at the American University in Cairo. He kneeled down and put his arms around his family—around Giovanni, Alessandro, and a one-year-old Isabella cradled in Michele's arms—then bowed his head low and wept.

Until the very end, he quietly kept tabs on all his nieces and nephews, following the lives of Giovanni, Alessandro, Isabella and Cezanne, forever consulting with his mother and sisters about their wellbeing and hopes for the future. Over the years, Michele kept the hearth warm for Daniel. When duty allowed, he would stop by her house to embrace the kids, forever renewing the tears of his regret for the pain of time lost.

In the many and various ways in which each of us are called, those who serve the common good pay a high price, as do their families.

Dark Sayings

Daniel found comfort in Michele's concern for his family during his travels, especially in later years, when the demands of his job left little opportunity for connection with loved ones. Michele's hospitality towards his wife, Renae, and her family, became ever more crucial as his health failed.

Daniel loved Renae. Their marriage of twenty-three years was the fulfillment of his testimony to his mother and sisters: that Renae was his soul mate and the love of his life, the place his heart found intimate kinship. Their commitment to each other, and Daniel's love for her mother Claudette and her whole family, are a memory of immeasurable value to be cherished and lived.

Dearest Renae, we give thanks for the life you shared with Daniel. No words can fill the emptiness of your sorrow, save the Lord's wisdom, which opens our eyes to the beauty that Daniel saw in others—the beauty he saw in you. Daniel was moved by the Scripture readings that you and your siblings shared at your father's funeral. I pray that we have done the same for your husband. Your love, the gift of so fortunate a marriage, made Daniel's life possible. May his memory and the bond of love that drew you together be eternal.

Daniel was born with a heart murmur. Marcia and Daniel Sr. spent many sleepless nights knowing that their little boy might not make it to adulthood.

Dearest Marcia, none of us understand the pain of your loss. As an elder mother, you are a sacred presence in our community, a biblical sign of the merciful womb that bore us in the church of our youth. None of us can comfort you in your loss, nor will I speak the empty words of vain men, that "no mother should see her son die."

I will not speak it and you will not allow it, for how many mothers have lost their sons to violence or poverty?

No. For you, it is the will of God that fills your sorrow with the hope of his teaching for the next generation. The teaching you whispered into Daniel's ear as you nursed him. Even now, this wisdom nourishes countless people you've never met. Now, it is Daniel's legacy that lingers. May the knowledge of this truth fill your days with meaning.

What I remember most is the Daniel of my youth. The brother who served with me at the Lord's altar. The Daniel who once gave me his liturgical robe to save me from embarrassment; the boy who always rushed to encourage others. The young man who walked to church early every week to assist my grandfather.

I see the same values at work in Daniel's nephew, Hayden, who, like his uncle, stands by me at the altar. In a twist of fate stranger than fiction, in the very same neighborhood.

To you, Hayden, I now speak the words of Maya Angelou on your uncle's lips, a call to arms from beyond the grave:

"Nothing will work unless you do."

Just as you did on this most important day, your uncle stood before the sacred step at St. Elizabeth's and proclaimed to all the Epistle of St. Paul in letters divinely inscribed:

> *"For the word of the cross is foolishness to those who are perishing, but to us who are being saved it is the power of God. For it is written, 'I will destroy the wisdom of the wise, and the cleverness of the clever I will thwart.'" (1 Corinthians 1:18)*

Daniel and I were two kids from a scrappy little church long since gone, like the towns and villages its founders left behind. Two kids from the West Side, from an immigrant and minority community, mostly invisible and seemingly unimportant, in an era when religion and our Arab roots remain the butt of the joke. But we both shared something powerful in common:

We were not ashamed.

In time, our pride, the meaning of those days, and its moral imperative would shape our respective paths:

> *"For consider your call, brethren; not many of you were wise according to worldly standards, not many were powerful, not many were of noble birth; but God chose what is foolish in the world to shame the wise, God chose what is weak in the world to shame the strong, God chose what is low and despised in the world, even the things that are not, to bring to nothing the things that are, so that no human being might boast in the presence of God." (1 Corinthians 1:26-29)*

> *"Let him who boasts, boast in the Lord." (1 Corinthians 26:31)*

Daniel, in Hebrew, means "God is my judge," a name handed down to him from his paternal grandmother,

Stand Your Ground

Refujia, whose name, in Spanish, means "refuge." We commit our brother Daniel to the merciful Lord, our compassionate judge, who is present to us in the death of human might and prestige.

MAY THIS GOD, our heavenly Father, grant our brother Daniel rest in the bosom of Abraham, together with our Lord Jesus Christ and all the saints, who from age to age have been our refuge and help; through the grace and compassion of his all-holy, good, and life-creating Spirit; now and always, in the hope of his Everlasting Kingdom. Amen.

CHRIST IS IN OUR MIDST

72

---

72 The calligraphy weaves the Arabic, *taʿāyush* (from *ʿāsh*, "to live") and the modern Hebrew, *du-kiyum* into a depiction of God's earth. Both words refer to the peaceful cohabitation of different groups in the same locality. In modern Hebrew, *du* (from the Latin, *duo*) means "two." *kiyum* is derived from the same root as the biblical triliteral *qum* (Arabic, *qāma*) which means to "stand out." The same root is found in God's promise in Genesis, "**I** will *establish (haqimoti)* **my covenant** with you," for the continuation of life. (6:18); Gabriel Wolff, "Coexistence" in Arabic and Hebrew.; hebrew-tattoos.com and pinterest.com/pin/14707136272825154.

Bread and Stone

"People are not, for example, terribly anxious to be equal (equal, after all, to what and to whom?), but they love the idea of being superior." —James Baldwin, The Fire Next Time

The interplay between the terms *bayt* and *heykal* in biblical Hebrew is simple. So simple that it can be explained to a child. A *heykal* is a building made of stone that serves as both a temple and a palace for the king. The writers of the old TV series Stargate SG1 got the basic premise correct. People are fooled into worshiping their leaders as gods—and the bloody Pharaohs didn't even have to be aliens. Just ordinary humans. That's how gullible we are. Wear some flashy gold bling; execute a few poor people; build a shiny tower with your name on it, and everyone thinks you are the bomb.

It is so simple. Yet we persist in pushing against it. We insist on our own agendas and human dynasties because deep down inside, we love Pharaoh and want to be like him.

Even your Anglo-Saxon nursery rhymes are more honest than your false teachings and your lying teachers:

"Here's the church, and here's the steeple. Open the door and see all the people."

It is the people for whom God cares, not your steeples, your towers of Babel:

"Then they said, 'Come, let us build ourselves a city and a tower with its top in the heavens, and let us make a name for

Bread and Stone

ourselves, otherwise, we will be scattered abroad over the face of the whole earth.'" (Genesis 11:4)

Thanks be to the God of Scripture that he hears neither you nor your false teachers, the "growers" and "builders." Instead, the Lord puts his words on the lips of his preachers, who smash your towers, scattering his children "abroad over the face of the whole earth," in the skillful care of *his* wisdom, according to the integrity of *his* heart, guided by *his* skillful hands in *his* Kingdom under the heavens.

Dung Piles

(Homily, Sunday, July 23, 2023)

In the name of the Father, and of the Son, and of the Holy Spirit. Amen.

Christ is in our Midst!

I had a lovely chat yesterday with Michele and her daughter, Isabella, who is working on her doctorate in psychology. We were chatting about institutional profiteering and its disastrous constraints on patient prognoses.

A prognosis is a deity, a form of human judgment, a Platonism, by which we fashion a god of flesh in the mind of a suffering person, unleashing tyranny.

Such gods are typical of religion and psychology, where a child of God's household comes to you in pain, burdened with a trauma of some kind, whatever the cause.

Under the pressure of need motivated by the love of money, you are forced to come up with an explanation that benefits your institution, not the person. In a religious setting, whatever will keep them in church; in a clinic, whatever will satisfy the insurance company's requirements or legal anxieties—all of which jeopardize the most vulnerable of God's people.

You, O David, are the slave of God, commissioned to protect his people, not to serve your *teraphim*.

You have no clue what's going on in that person's life, but somehow, in thirty minutes, your task is to theologize, to guess at a prognosis. To blabber on the air in a vacuum, like Frasier: the wise sage of idiots and pleasure-seekers.

Such is human judgment.

You create a false god and impose it on a person in need—you put your idea in their head. Your fabrication makes matters worse for them because they believe you. They trust in you. Your placebo takes on a life of its own, and "the last deception" becomes much "worse than the first." (Matthew 27:64)

> *"Jesus answered and said to them, "Those who are well have no need of a physician, but those who are sick. I have not come to call the righteous, but sinners, to repentance." (Luke 5:31-32)*

Beloved in Christ, we Americans are fat, dumb, and happy. Our wealth has led us to moral bankruptcy and extreme self-involvement. Yes, this creates a kind of psychological suffering, but this is no credit to us.

Bread and Stone

This kind of suffering is self-inflicted, wrought by disobedience. It is the type that prevents us from seeing the needs of others. This suffering has its own, Satanic temperament. It remembers the wound and urges the privileged and comfortable to think only of themselves as they punch down. The kind of suffering that separates Americans from the love of God and each other.

So, we walk around in a coma, without empathy, blind to the suffering of others. We are the ones in need of a prognosis. Say this aloud in the churches, I dare you. Tell those who have everything that they are nothing in God's eyes. Tell them something is wrong with them and see them spit on you as they walk away, in fulfillment of the Prophets:

"For if anyone thinks he is something when he is nothing, he deceives himself." (Galatians 6:3)

But when someone with actual trauma is in pain, be cautious with your prognosis. Reassure them, fearing God's will, and love them, but do not put your god in their head.

Keep your opinions to yourself.

Be caring and supportive, by all means, and let them talk, but keep your gods at bay because neither you nor they are the judge, unlike your insurance companies and stewardship programs who rush the prognosis to fatten the tariff.

And when you open your mouth to console a person in need, let not one syllable—not an iota or a dot—stray from what is written in Scripture because:

Dark Sayings

"For every careless word that people speak, they will give an account on the day of judgment." (Matthew 12:36)

Beloved in Christ:

As the deacon said this morning, according to St. Paul, Scripture puts pressure on those who are strong:

"We who are strong are obligated to bear the weaknesses of those without strength and not to seek our own pleasure." (Romans 15:1)

"We who are strong."

We are the ones, from the perspective of the Prophets, to whom the psychologist and the priest must say:

It is you who are not right in the head!

But in our institutionalized and "civilized" system, everything is backward. We put pressure on the weak and the sick, shaming and punishing them while holding banquets for wealthy donors. We pontificate about the "sins" of the homeless, drug addicts, and disenfranchised while applauding and congratulating people who are doing just fine.

It's a big joke.

My conversation with Marcia's granddaughter is an opportunity to say, once again, that Scripture is anti-institutional and, as such, is unacceptable to American Christians.

American Christians come to church with their own program and agenda in mind.

What they want.

Bread and Stone

What they plan to do.

Their plan is neither the program nor the agenda encoded in God's *zera'*; (seed). As Paul says:

"Each person is to remain in that state in which he was called." (1 Corinthians 7:20)

I have been chanting the Psalms in this neighborhood since I was a ten-year-old, walking to Vespers—back in the good old days when we could go outside and walk around or ride bikes without safety helmets and helicopter surveillance. I operate the same way today as a priest as I did back then, and I will not change—because Scripture is the work God put in me to do.

This is what I am telling you:

No expansion, no growth, no buildings, no empires, no legacy, none of it. I am not interested in any of it. I am interested in doing what I have done all along, chanting the Psalms aloud for you until I cannot.

We are commanded not to change because the seed is all that matters and does not belong to us. If we submit to the seed, we are imprisoned with the Apostle Paul to do the will:

Not of family or friends,
Nor of the church,
Nor of the society,

But of God the Father, through Jesus Christ our Lord. We have one responsibility for the sake of the poor: to keep reciting his words, the *debarim* of God.

Period.

Dark Sayings

The unfortunate situation for us in the New Testament is that we are stuck in the Roman Empire, which means that we are stuck with buildings and human systems.

Along these lines, I was explaining to Marcia's children a beautiful metaphor that Father Timothy Lowe shared with me during my personal trials a couple of years ago:

"The dung pile."

It is a wonderful metaphor. Just think about it. How many of you have been to the State Fair? Or the Renaissance Festival? Alla (*Im Nadim*) [73] loves the Renaissance Festival.

You go to the festival, and everywhere you look, you find animal feces, dung piles. Kathy and George are farmers. They understand. The dung pile is gross. Forget the suburbs where people walk around with "pooper scoopers." You only need a pooper scooper because, as Chrysostom said, you poured out a pavement.[74]

In the wilderness, there is no need for a pooper scooper. An animal does its business and keeps walking.

---

[73] In Arabic, *Nadim* means friend, confidant, or companion; pourer of wine; table fellow in the company of elders.

[74] When at capacity, the Burj Khalifa is estimated to produce seven tons of poop daily with no direct connection to municipal sewage. "Trucks often wait in line for up to 24 hours before they can offload their payload."; Meinhold, Bridgette. "The Incredible Story of How the Burj Khalifa's Poop Is Trucked Out of Town." Inhabitat, Dec. 2021, inhabitat.com/the-incredible-story-of-how-the-burj-khalifas-poop-is-trucked-out-of-town.

Bread and Stone

You know the animal was there because it left a trace, but eventually, the wind blows, rain falls, and the dung pile disappears. It stinks for a bit, but eventually, it is gone. More than that, it fertilizes the ground as God intended, and something beautiful grows in its place.

When a Bedouin tribe sets up camp, they have tents. So, there is civilization, but in time the tents come down. When they leave, the only waste left over is biological. It all returns to the dust after a few days or weeks. The same was true for traditional Native American society. In Palestine, before 1918, local families shared 70% of God's land in common:[75]

> *"And all the believers were together and had all things in common; and they would sell their property and possessions and share them with all, to the extent that anyone had need." (Acts 2:44-45)*

> *"And the congregation of those who believed were of one heart and soul; and not one of them claimed that anything belonging to him was his own, but all things were common property to them." (Acts 4:32)*

This practice, known as *mushaʻa*, only ended when the British, in their extreme colonial hubris, felt it was

---

[75] "According to S. Ilan Troen (Professor of Israel Studies at Brandeis University) 70% of the land in Palestine was *mushaʻa* in 1918. Kenneth W. Stein says that by 1923 *mushaʻa* lands had been reduced to around half the lands under the British colonial regime in Mandatory Palestine. By 1946 only 20% of the lands were *mushaʻa*."; Wikipedia contributors. "Musha Land." *Wikipedia*, Feb. 2023, en.wikipedia.org/wiki/Musha_land.

Dark Sayings

necessary to take over for God—and they labeled it "progess."[76]

Nomadic life in Scripture is the Scriptural paradigm for living. That is the teaching that I keep repeating to you and have been chanting in this neighborhood since I was ten years old:

> *"As for man, his days are like grass; Like a flower of the field, so he flourishes. When the wind has passed over it, it is no more, and its place no longer knows about it. But the mercy of the Lord is from everlasting to everlasting for those who fear him, and his justice to the children's children, to those who keep his covenant and remember his precepts, so as to do them." (Psalm 103:15–18)*

That is what Matthew is referring to in his admonition about the lilies of the field. The lilies blossom and then die, and no one remembers the place where they were. Meanwhile, Solomon, who in all his glory[77] will never be as beautiful as a fleeting flower, ran a stupid rat race to

---

[76] "The British and the Zionists saw the [peasants'] inability to sell lands as an impediment to progress." In such peasant (*fallāḥīn*) tribal families, a brother, mother, or sister found their value and purpose within the *mushaʻa* social hierarchy. Compare this to the Melting Pot, which eradicates family hierarchy and history upon entry, leaving everyone to self-identify based on the car they drive, the size and location of their house, and their job title.; Kimmerling, Baruch. *The Palestinian People: A History.* Harvard UP, 2009, p 18.

[77] (Matthew 6:29) The queen of the south (Hebrew, *sheba*, Arabic, *saba*) will rise in judgment (Matthew 12:42) because when she came to Solomon for wisdom, he took her gold and sent her packing. (1 Kings 10:1-21; 2 Chronicles 9:1-20) *Sheba* is a people and a kingdom in southern Arabia (Yemen region) in the Bible and the Qur'an noted for its wealth.

Bread and Stone

win a game of thrones for a legacy that ended in civil war, ashes, and destruction.

Do you get it yet?

No one remembers the Algonquian tribes or the families of the *musha'a*. They are gone. But God's mercy and compassion, expressed in childbirth, ensure the continuation of the life he gave them for the generations yet unborn, to be shepherded and cared for by the seed of his wisdom.

That is our duty. Share and share alike. Pay it forward. It does not belong to you!

When the house of St. Elizabeth—the *people* of St. Elizabeth are God's house! When God's house moved into this physical building—made by the hand of man—the biggest concern that Dan and Larry had was the risk of residual toxins in a structure built at the end of the nineteenth century.

We knew nothing about the people who lived here. We had to do research to learn about them—about the Lord's household dwelling here before us. They were gone. What did they teach? Who were they?

All that remained was a structure poisoning the earth, which could poison us. So, we worked to remove those toxins from the structure.

Consider what I am saying.

I had to search the Internet and immigration records to learn more about the German immigrants who sojourned here. St. Elizabeth, incidentally, was German by birth.

Dark Sayings

They were Volga Germans (*Wolgadeutsche*) "Russian Germans" (*Povolzhskiye nemtsy*) who came here in 1894 from colonies along the Volga River in the south, near Ukraine.[78] Members of the Deutsche Volkskirche, the "German Peoples Church," and eventually, the Riverview Peoples Church—a parish that disappeared here sometime during or after World War II. We know from the historical record that many of its members transferred to a nearby Lutheran community[79] as early as 1936.[80]

They became Lutherans—the only people in Minnesota to help my childhood parish financially when its building was destroyed by fire.

Such is the House of God, the Body of Jesus Christ, not this temple of "cedar and stone" made by human hands.

Do you think this building means anything? Can you find these people anywhere today? We barely know the

---

[78] Wikipedia contributors. "Volga Germans." *Wikipedia*, July 2023, en.wikipedia.org/wiki/Volga_Germans.
[79] "Deutsche Volkskirche." *The Volga Germans*, www.volgagermans.org/who-are-volga-germans/history /immigration/united-states/minnesota/st-paul/deutsche-volkskirche. Accessed 31 May 2023.
[80] "Deutsche Volkskirche (Riverview Peoples Church) - St. Paul." *Volga German Institute*, volga.domains.unf.edu/congregations/deutsche-volkskirche-riverview-peoples-church-st-paul. Accessed 31 May 2023.

Bread and Stone

names of their pastors, let alone the many pastors and households who came after them.[81]

---

[81] The West Side is a haven for immigrant communities arriving in St. Paul, Minnesota. Historically, it has included people of German, Roma, Polish, Swedish, Irish, Jewish (fleeing Russian pogroms), Latin American, Middle Eastern (among them after 1948, Palestinians) and African heritage. It is a place where different languages, religions, and cultures coexist in the womb of God's earth without colonial integration, though not free from its ire. The latter is felt in the absence of the native Mdewakanton Dakota people, who sojourned locally along the river in a seasonal encampment under a succession of chiefs known as "Little Crow." After Minnesota became a territory in 1849, colonial merchants were eager to "expand" and "build" bigger "barns." (Luke 12:16-21) So, by 1851, the nomadic tribes of God were driven out of nearly all of Elohim's earth in Minnesota and eastern Dakota in the Traverse des Sioux and Mendota treaties. The same colonial resentments resurfaced first in the suppression of the German language by the "Minnesota Commision of Public Safety," and later in the 1930s during the Great Depression, when, in several attempts to address the "Mexican problem," Ramsey County officials repatriated no less than 15% of the Mexican population, many of whom were U.S. citizens. "This was the West Side Flats, and for about a hundred years, from the 1850s to the 1960s, life bloomed there. A unique neighborhood in Minnesota and the wider U.S., the Flats were dense, low-income, polyglot, striving, unpaved, and unpainted." In this sense, despite its material (and at times extreme) poverty and because of its mix of languages under constant outside pressure, it is reminiscent of al-Andalus, the fleeting memory of a golden age of tolerance, cultural exchange, and common sense. Despite regular flooding in the old neighborhood, city officials did nothing to address the issue or assist West Side residents. Only after the demolition of the Flats and the deportation (integration into the Melting Pot) of its residents in 1963 did the "community builders" of Ramsey County install flood

Dark Sayings

Daliya and I had a beautiful conversation in the car on the way to church today. We listened to the congressional hearings on the unionization of Starbucks employees. Bernie Sanders was presiding. As a man of Scripture, I do not agree with anyone, but if I must choose, Bernie Sanders is my kind of American because he does not change. He stands his ground. He will not give up the fight on behalf "of those without strength." In this regard, he is old school, like figures from my childhood who disappeared into this age—only Bernie Sanders did not disappear.[82] So, I respect him. He and I

---

control mechanisms on the Riverfront. "What they did to the Mexicans down on the old West Side—to make them move like that, and not compensate them, and give them the bare minimum. What they did to destroy a community like that is wrong." — George Avaloz; *West Side Flats, St. Paul | MNopedia.* www.mnopedia.org/place/west-side-flats-st-paul,; *Kaposia Indian Site - Mississippi National River and Recreation Area (U.S. National Park Service).* www.nps.gov/miss/planyourvisit /kapoindi .htm; "West Side History." *West Side Community Organization,* www.wsco .org/westsidehistory.; Becker, Jessica. "1851 Treaty of Traverse des Sioux." *Nicollet County Historical Society,* Sept. 2021, www.nchsmn.org/1851-treaty-of-traverse-des-sioux.; "The West Side Flats." *West Side Community Organization,* www.wsco.org/ west_side_flats.; Alam, Ehsan. "During World War I, Minnesota Nativists Waged an All Out War on German Culture in the State." *MinnPost,* 5 Jan. 2016, minnpost.com/mnopedia/2016/01/during-world-war-i-minnesota-nativists-waged-all-out-war-german-cultur e-state/;Roethke, Leigh. *Latino Minnesota.* Minnesota Historical Society, 2009, pp. 40-41.

[82] Whatever Sanders believes, his actions demonstrate the Torah written on his heart. The wealthy, the corporate media, and his own party turned against him, a scriptural sign (at the age of eighty-one!) that he remains on the correct path.; BBC Newsnight. "Noam

Bread and Stone

breathe the same air. But I disagree with him because I do not believe in the system. I believe in the Scriptural God.

In any case, as to be expected (as though we are all still in high school debate), the argument devolved into those who are pro and anti-union.

The funny thing is that people who believe in the system make sound arguments on all sides, but all their arguments are in vain because they are predicated on a lie. You cannot make something out of a dung pile.

This sounds horrible until you submit to the beauty of God's teaching—to the wonder of his Creation in Ecclesiastes, where he explains that we are no different from animals. We all share the same breath:

"For the fate of the sons of men and the fate of animals is the same. As one dies, so dies the other; indeed, they all have the same breath, and there is no advantage for man over animal, for all is vanity. All go to the same place. All came from the dust, and all return to the dust." (Ecclesiastes 3:19–20)

Like the other animals, God created us to make a small stink and then move on. This sounds bad and improper in your Anglo-Saxon ears because you still do not realize that we, the men and women of colonial civilization, make artificial dung piles of much worse composition. Toxic dung piles with forever chemicals that do not biodegrade and are full of leftover materials

---

Chomsky: I Would Vote for Jeremy Corbyn (Extended Interview) - BBC Newsnight." *YouTube*, 10 May 2017, www.youtube.com/watch?v=edicDsSwYpk.

that cause cancer. Composites that hurt people, animals, and vegetation.

The point is not to abandon civilization, though if you can, God bless you:

> *"For…if you speak of exile, you mention that which only involves a change of country and the sight of many cities, or if you speak of confiscation of goods, you mention what is only freedom and emancipation from care." (St. John Chrysostom, Letter to Olympias)*[83]

It is not impossible, though colonialism and surveillance capitalism are making it much more difficult for nomadic peoples.

The point of the New Testament is to *inhabit the place* wherein *you are found* with the mentality of a nomadic household.

We *must* accept the teaching of St. Paul as our reference. Paul is sometimes our *paterfamilias* and, at other times, our *oikonomos*, but in God's Roman household, *always* our point of reference. This household, co-opted in his epistles, is best understood against the backdrop of Bedouin shepherd life, which is nomadic and transient.

Even though you are stuck with the trappings of the Roman Empire, with cities, power structures, and the like, wherever you find yourself remains the flesh-and-blood household, which belongs not to Caesar but to God, your heavenly Father. So, stay as you are but place

---

[83] Barry, Jennifer. *Bishops in Flight: Exile and Displacement in Late Antiquity.* University of California Press, 2019, p. 76.

your trust in God and not in Rome, its leaders, structures, or systems.

"Put not your trust in princes, in sons of men, in whom there is no salvation." (Psalm 146:3)

Because when I hear a highly educated Ivy League graduate speaking on behalf of Starbucks, explaining and expounding the value of corporate teamwork against the corrosive potential of unions, I hear "we who are strong" punching down against the weak in defense of some stupid high-minded, virtuous ideal masking corporate greed. That is what Father Paul means by "NATO theology."

On the other side of the aisle, when I hear the downtrodden argue in his own defense that we must fight against corruption and establish a union to defend the weak, I hear the oppressed and persecuted Jew who saw six million of our brothers and sisters brutally exterminated by the Nazis already setting his sights on another people's homeland.

Nothing changes under the sun.

Until we accept the truth of Scripture, that God alone is our Judge and *we are the villains* of history, the oppressed will forever rise up as oppressors.

There is no God but Elohim, and Jesus is his prophet, the Suffering Servant of Isaiah, whom he raised from the dead and seated at his right hand as King, Son of God, and Messiah, coming in power *to oppress us through his teaching,* so that no human being may boast in the presence of God!

Dark Sayings

Yet, each time I turn on the television or browse the web, I hear people boasting on all sides.

Listen carefully to the text of the liturgy. The body of Christ is broken. And whose body are we? The House of Israel in a Roman setting is the body politic of the Republic. That is what we preach when we proclaim the breaking of the Eucharistic bread!

Beloved in Christ, something broken cannot assert itself!

This is why I roll my eyes when people say we are all equal; we are all the same. No, you are not all equal; you are all broken and repeatedly scattered in the Old Testament! You are all suppressed so that only One, who is holy, stands out!

Since I was a child, I have listened to the children of the sixties, the most exceptionalistic in a long line of exceptional Americans, preach egalitarianism and equality.

They are lying.

No matter what Leylah does, she will never be Karima's equal. It is impossible because, as God wills, Karima[84] is the opener of the womb. This is not a moral question. It is a fact.

---

[84] Our firstborn child. In Arabic, *Karima* means generous, magnanimous, noble, and openhanded but also precious and costly. In Scripture, "precious stones" *hijāratun karīmatun*. (Isaiah 54:12; 1 Corinthians 3:12)

Bread and Stone

Sons and daughters of Plato, I do not care if you agree with me. Disagree at your own peril. I do not belong to you. I am a son of the commandment.

Once you realize that philosophical equality is the mental construct of colonial slave owners, it follows that not all words are equal:

"For my thoughts are not your thoughts, neither are your ways my ways, declares Yahweh." (Isaiah 55:8)

If you submit to Yahweh, you must accept that his words are not equal to yours. Logically, it follows that the one whom God assigns to speak his words, whomever that is, even if it is a sixteen-year-old Jeremiah, in his function, is not your equal.

In the end, like all those who serve the common good, this one is discarded and cursed, like a used-up oblation hanging from the side of the Temple wall.

If you do not believe me look upon the one hanging naked—he is not naked in your icon—but in Scripture, he is fully naked, hanging in shame and defeat on the Cross.

That is Elohim's teaching, which is why your Jeffersonian equality is anti-scriptural. You call it equality. You say everyone is the same.

"Everyone puts their pants on the same way, Father Marc."

In truth, you mean, "I am the king of my own castle; I can do and say whatever I want, so leave me alone, and please do not tell me what to do; it is my life."

Dark Sayings

Well, if you cannot be told what to do, dear friends, then you are gods, sons of the Most High, all of you.

Nevertheless, you will die like any man and fall like any prince.

Against you and me, I sing:

"Arise, O God, judge the earth! For to you belong all the nations." (Psalm 82:8)

CHRIST IS IN OUR MIDST

*"Lying, thinking
Last night
How to find my soul a home
Where water is not thirsty
And bread loaf is not stone
I came up with one thing
And I don't believe I'm wrong
That nobody,
But nobody
Can make it out here alone.*

*Alone, all alone
Nobody, but nobody
Can make it out here alone.*

*There are some millionaires
With money they can't use
Their wives run round like banshees
Their children sing the blues
They've got expensive doctors
To cure their hearts of stone.
But nobody
No, nobody
Can make it out here alone.*

*Alone, all alone
Nobody, but nobody
Can make it out here alone.*

*Now if you listen closely
I'll tell you what I know
Storm clouds are gathering
The wind is gonna blow
The race of man is suffering
And I can hear the moan,
'Cause nobody,
But nobody
Can make it out here alone.*

*Alone, all alone
Nobody, but nobody
Can make it out here alone."*

—Maya Angelou, Alone

On August 25, 2023, on St. Paul's West Side, on the corner of Clinton and Congress St. E., across the way from El Rio Vista, down by the Neighborhood House near the Paul and Sheila Wellstone Center, where kids still play outside near Parque de Castillo, against the unforgiving edge of the colonial Melting Pot, international scholars from the Middle East (and other continents) gathered together to bear witness: The gospel of the Lord's Christ to the poor was carried to the people of the West Side. Fr. Paul Nadim Tarazi delivered the paper:

> *"Multiple readings of the sacred text throughout history. Is it enrichment or a cause of conflict? Biblical criticism and date of receipt of the text."*

A lifetime of effort encoded in a but a sentence. An English translation of the original paper delivered in Arabic on March 15, 2023, before the Third Conference for the Sacred Texts: Controversies in Christianity and Islam. The conference was organized by the Saint Joseph University of Beirut and the Bible Society of Lebanon, in cooperation with the Institute for Abrahamic Relations.

> *"He who has ears to hear, let him hear."*
> *(Mark 4:9)*

www.ingramcontent.com/pod-product-compliance
Lightning Source LLC
Chambersburg PA
CBHW050013090426
42734CB00020B/3255